London 19th 1992.

TROLLOPE

Darling Woona,

Graeme & Helen will
deliver this to you with
my fondest love. I hope
the text is as good as the
illustrations! See you soon,
darling.

Hennie X

1815–1882

C. P. SNOW

TROLLOPE

THE HERBERT PRESS

Copyright © C. P. Snow 1975
Copyright under the Berne Convention

First edition 1975

This paperback edition first published in Great Britain 1991
by The Herbert Press Ltd, 46 Northchurch Road, London N1 4EJ
Published by arrangement with Rainbird Publishing Group Limited

Printed and bound in Hong Kong by
South China Printing Co. (1988) Ltd

A CIP catalogue record for this book is available
from the British Library.

ISBN 1–871569–41–9

CONTENTS

LIST OF COLOUR PLATES

NOTE: *The page numbers given are those opposite the colour plates, or, in the case of a double page spread, those either side of the plate*

PREFACE

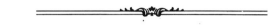

Trollope's novels will offer plenty of opportunities to scholars for a long time to come. So far the surface has only been skimmed. This probably isn't true of the factual details of his life. It would be a surprise if much new material was now discovered. He had his secrets, but they were secrets of his inner self. There is little in the shape of documents, except those – his autobiography among them – which he deliberately controlled. We have to make do with what there is, and do our best with our own interpretations.

However, in the course of writing this book, it has been possible to fill in some factual gaps. Unpublished letters of Trollope's are still being accumulated by the Morris L. Parrish collection of the Princeton University Library and, through the generosity of Alexander D. Wainwright, the curator, these have been available for study. There are now over two hundred, in addition to a number of fragments, dated from 1839 to the last year of Trollope's life. They do not substantially alter previous impressions or biographical statements, but in places they strengthen or confirm them (compare chapter 19, and notes to that chapter).

Investigation of Post Office records has produced some interesting results. There have been suggestions that Trollope's claim to have initiated the letterbox is not well founded. That would have been utterly out of character, and is untrue. The Post Office documents tell the whole story, as Mrs J. Y. Farrugia has already demonstrated (see chapter 9 and note 1 to that chapter). Whatever Government Departments don't do, they do keep records.

Thanks to the knowledge and friendly services of Mrs Farrugia, Assistant Curator of the Postal Museum, and also those of Mrs C. McNamara, of Post Office Records, other features of Trollope's official career have, from the documentary evidence, been cleared up. The entire circumstances of his not being appointed in 1864 to the Assistant Secretaryship at the Post Office, which he dearly wanted, can be followed almost day by day (compare chapter 15).

Other debts of gratitude are owed to – Professor J. H. Plumb, for advice on historical and biographical procedure, Peter Faure of George Rainbird Ltd, for indefatiguable editorial help, Charles Scribner, Jr, Burroughs Mitchell, Jacques Barzun, of Charles Scribner's Sons, New York, for detailed textual scrutiny, and to the staff of the London Library.

London   C.P.S.
8 April 1975

1
BORN A GENTLEMAN

All through his childhood and youth Anthony Trollope was more loving than loved. Somewhere deep in his nature this – what shall we call it? longing? deprivation? – lasted all his life. It may have been innate, one of the unfortunate gifts of fate, like his short sight or his heavy lumbering physique. We who read him with delight and admiration nearly a hundred years after his death, which would have astonished him, since he was the most modest of great writers, can be grateful for his bad luck. It probably helped endow him with the specific insight, the delicate fluid empathy, which made him the finest natural psychologist of all nineteenth-century novelists. It certainly made it necessary for him to build his character, curiously structured between the over-sensitive interior and the bluff, sturdy, honourable, plain-dealing outside, one of his own grandest creations.

All this will come into the story of his life and art. Whether he would have been happier if he had been better loved as a child is anyone's guess, and it is not much use speculating. Conventional psychologists would say yes. He probably wouldn't have done. He took an altogether more sombre and more realistic view of human destiny. He didn't believe that there were easy or hygienic answers.

However, there is no doubt at all that he went through a childhood and youth which most of us would shrink from. This is painful to think of, even if we read his own account, as we should, with a certain amount of caution. It was written in old age (a premature old age by our standards), and, though he was as honest as a man can reasonably be, he was cheering himself up by thinking of his life as a kind of fairy-tale story, Ugly Duckling or Cinderella, you can take your choice. We shall have to return to that point, for so much of the traditional picture of Trollope[1] derives from his own works; there is very little, genuinely original and independent, which comes from others.

It was a miserable childhood, when any reservations are made. It is hard to think of any good writer who had as wretched a time and had to

Russell Square. The houses in Keppel Street would have been not unlike this

endure it for so long. By comparison, Dickens's experience in the black-ing factory was an episode, and Dostoevsky, shut up in the claustro-phobic apartment of a Moscow hospital doctor, had a relatively ebul-lient boyhood.[2] Trollope's had sustained patches of sustained wretched-ness, so far as a vigorous boy can sustain wretchedness which in an acceptant temperament like his was too long. We had better begin there.

Trollope was born at 16 Keppel Street in Waterloo year, 1815. You can still find Keppel Street if you walk north up Tottenham Court Road, take the third turning right along Store Street, and go straight along. There is nothing left, though, of the Trollopes' Keppel Street. In their time it contained terraces of neat Georgian houses, houses of barristers, clergymen, the professional upper middle class. The houses would have been fairly new. It is interesting that neither Trollope nor his older brother Tom had the slightest feeling for Georgian architecture. It was their contemporary style, they being born in the reign of George III, and they thought it excessively plain and dull.

If you want to know what the Trollopes' house looked like, you have only to go round the corner into Gower Street. These narrow-fronted houses are relics of what prosperous professional families lived in. They lived according to a standard pattern, dining room on the ground floor, main drawing room on the floor above, both giving onto the street. This was a practical arrangement which has been maintained to this day by people who can afford private houses of this size. (They usually have more rooms than one would expect.)

When Trollope was a boy, the family dinner downstairs presented some revealing features. It took place later than was customary, usually about five in the afternoon.[3] This was because Mr Trollope, himself a barrister like many of his neighbours, was obsessively conscientious: though he hadn't much work to do in his chambers in Lincoln's Inn, he stayed a long time over it. The food would strike a modern observer as depressingly plain and monotonous. That wouldn't have distinguished it from food in other such houses round about. The Georgian upper bourgeoisie lived to a large extent on mutton. What would have distinguished it from other such houses was that the candles were tallow, not wax. Tallow candles were cheaper. Mr Trollope, in a state of gloomy bafflement, was doing increasingly badly at the Bar.

Poor food in the dark room. But what would also surprise a modern observer, they were served by a young man-servant in livery. In the Trollope livery, for, though they might have descended into the shabby genteel, the Trollopes were an authentically well-connected family. One relative, not so distant, carried the title of the Trollope baronetcy, which had been granted in the seventeenth century.

Trollope's eldest brother, Tom, writing three-quarters of a century after this Keppel Street period, remarked that for such a family at that time a servant in livery was not an affectation. It would have been unthinkable, or at least unconventional, not to have him on view. On the other hand, it would have been even more unthinkable to put him into livery to which the family were not entitled. Rank still meant something in Regency England, and a good deal later than that. The Trollopes might be getting steadily more impoverished, but they were gentlefolk.

The young Trollope, soon after the family left Keppel Street, was going to be weighed down by twenty years of neglect and humiliation. Quite often, during that stretch of servitude, he seems to have had only one support. A frail support at any time, one would have thought, and unavailable in the world which was coming and which in old age he didn't much like, yet it was a support to him. He could tell himself that, after all, he was a gentleman.[4]

Gentleman here, in the typical English muddle of formality and virtue, had two meanings. It meant the purely documentary fact that one's ancestor had at some previous time obtained a grant of arms from the College of Heralds. Thus the family became duly armigerous. This wasn't difficult. The Heralds were entitled to charge a fee when they gave a grant of arms, which disposed them not to be too pernickety. As we know, Shakespeare, a working actor, obtained arms for his father, apparently without much trouble, and thus was himself described in legal records as 'gentleman'. People have usually liked social gradations, particularly those who happen to be in, or reach, the upper ones.

To Trollope, though, there was quite another meaning. If one was born a gentleman, one was likely to be born to certain traits of character. Either by some mysterious inheritance or through training, one would try to live according to a code of probity, responsibility, uprightness. It is not clear how he rationalized this, but he certainly believed it to the end of his life, long after he needed that particular support for himself. He had no doubt that a gentleman was more suitable for a position of trust, as in the government service, than a chap who could pass examinations but who hadn't breathed this straightforward code as his native air.[5]

It sounds, to a late twentieth-century ear, intolerably snobbish. In a formal sense, he was so, as were all the Victorian writers one can think of, and all their predecessors from Shakespeare to Jane Austen and Walter Scott. In actual practice, his mixture of tolerance, warm-heartedness and unsentimental insight made him see individual men as they were, without trimmings. He was far less put off than Dickens by knockabout manners: compare their reactions to odd specimens of the American frontier.[6] He was utterly unimpressed by middle-class myths about the aristocracy, and the ruthless insight got to work on some of the biggest aristocratic crooks and vulgarians in all fiction – the de Courcys, Sowerby, Ralph Carberry, the Longstaffe sisters, very many more.

Nevertheless, it was important, specifically and articulately, to be a gentleman, as though he were clinging to that pathetic prop of his youth. At times he laughs at it, even in a conversation between Dalrymple and Johnny Eames,[7] the nearest approach to a self-portrait in all his corpus. At other times, he seems to believe, or want to believe, that the whole of English society can be divided into two great classes, gentlemen and non-gentlemen. Among gentlemen, there was no difference in rank. With his usual detachment, he points out that, when it comes to decisions, his great noblemen do not take precisely that attitude. The Duke of Omnium is a liberal, but he is shocked to the bone when he hears that young Tregear, penniless, a bit of an adventurer but unquestionably a gentleman, wants to marry a daughter[8] (rather like a theoretically liberal southern American hearing that the suitor is black).

His ecclesiastical characters do, however, subscribe to the Trollopian mystique. Archdeacon Grantly – content, rich, loving the world as it is – talks to Mr Crawley, half deranged, beset by tribulations, bringing up his family on a hundred and fifty a year. Mr Crawley's daughter is engaged to the Archdeacon's son. He says: 'I wish we stood on more equal grounds.' The Archdeacon replies: 'We stand on the only perfect level on which men can meet each other.' One might think this meant that they were both Christian priests. It doesn't. The Archdeacon continues: 'We are both gentlemen.'

Mr Crawley is dedicated to his religion, but he answers: 'Sir, from the bottom of my heart I thank you. I could not have spoken such words; but, coming from you who are rich to me who am poor they are honourable to the one and comfortable to the other.'[9]

How did members of this freemasonry recognize each other? Partly, of course, by manner, partly by education. The professional middle class was still small enough for them to know each other's school and college history. (Mr Crawley, despite his worldly failures, had had a distinguished career at Oxford.)

Even more, probably, by speech. This is an English peculiarity. Englishmen have been placing social origins by accent since the eighteenth century, and quite likely long before. How did they speak, that is, the Trollopes and their neighbours in Keppel Street, and, a generation later, Trollope's characters – parsons, lawyers, officials, country squires – and his friends at the Garrick?

To that we can give an answer with a fair degree of certainty. They spoke remarkably like their successors in similar positions today. We know this from several different lines of evidence. The dialogue in Trollope's own novels provides one. He happened to have an exceptionally good ear. He also listened with great care. From this work we can catch the tone of spoken professional English as from no other nineteenth-century writer. Some of the words have changed meaning. Some of the constructions have changed too: that will be discussed a little more fully later. But, in general, it is remarkable how steady the colloquial language of such people has remained. (This is not so true lower down the social scale.)

As for the sound of this nineteenth-century speech, we have to rely on oral evidence. That all points in the same direction. Aldous Huxley used to say that, if one wanted to know what the voices of his relatives in the eighties in cultivated Oxford sounded like, voices of children of T. H. Huxley, grandchildren of Thomas Arnold, you had only to listen to his own. Incidentally that was a beautiful way to speak the language. In the same fashion, it was possible in Oxford or Cambridge in the 1920s to listen to very old men, born in the 1850s, Fellows of colleges well before Trollope's death. One old man used to talk cheerfully of the last century, meaning the eighteenth. A few – not many – of the words they used struck strange, but the accent and intonation didn't. It was surprising to young listeners, a curious example of the continuity of one section of English society.[10]

This process of phonetic reconstruction might be carried further back. It is a reasonable guess that, transplanted to Keppel Street in 1815, before Queen Victoria was born, one would find the Trollopes' English almost immediately familiar, perhaps rather brisk and loud, for that was a Trollope characteristic, but far closer to modern educated English than is the language of modern professional footballers.

Mr and Mrs Trollope came from highly educated families. Both their fathers were clergymen, and both had been scholars of Winchester and Fellows of New College. This doesn't imply quite what it would today,[11] but they would certainly be cultivated late eighteenth-century High Churchmen, proficient Latinists, and, as we happen to know, given to intellectual interests. Mrs Trollope's father had also an endearing White Knight kind of inventiveness. He hated the noise of a knife squeaking on his plate, and spent much ingenuity devising a plate which didn't squeak.

In the autobiography Trollope says that, when he wrote the first of the Barchester novels, he had scarcely known an ecclesiastical dignitary.[12] That is no doubt factually true, in the sense that, at the time of *Barchester Towers*, he had never been intimate, or perhaps even casually friendly, with a Bishop or a Dean. But if interpreted to mean that he wasn't used to clergymen, that gives an impression which is dead wrong. Clerical visitors, even as the Trollopes became more penurious, were constantly in the house.

Transported to the Keppel Street dining room in 1815, the infant Trollope upstairs, we should find the English they spoke familiar and comforting. However, that would be about the only comforting feature in the establishment, apart perhaps from Mrs Trollope's high spirits. The trouble was Mr Trollope. Like his father and his father-in-law, he too had been a scholar at Winchester and a Fellow of New College. A little later, as his own ambitions came to nothing, his most passionate one was that his sons should do precisely the same. He was a man of considerable intelligence: in contemporary jargon, he had a high IQ. Like Mr Crawley, his son's most complex creation, he had had a brilliant career at Oxford. Like Mr Crawley – for it was with what must have been anguished study of his father that Trollope learned about a specific kind of temperament. Learned with such accuracy that there is nothing like such a clinical analysis in the whole of nineteenth-century fiction, not only English.

For shorthand purposes, it is convenient to use a technical label. Mr Trollope was, in his forties, progressing into a state of schizoid paranoia. This was shortly going to bring ruinous practical consequences. It also – as such a nature often does – induced acute anxiety, or angst to use another technical label, in everyone around him. His

This suggests Mr Trollope's methods of instruction to his family, though the father seems less irascible

eldest son Tom said that he never knew anyone enter his father's company who didn't want immediately to get out of it.[13] Trollope himself saw, with deep insight, what it was like to live in such a state. But even he, utterly unsentimental in dealing with Mr Crawley as with his other major characters, found it desirable to give him a spiritual aspiration – presumably to make him more acceptable – which from the available evidence Mr Trollope did not possess.

He did possess, in his unreachable schizoid ego, two certainties. The first was that, with his superior intellect and wisdom, he was always right. This didn't make him popular in negotiations with other lawyers.

[15]

His competence on paper no one disputed, but attorneys didn't like being hectored by this pedagogue of a man, and soon began to drop him. The second certainty, which followed on the first, was that all men were his enemies, determined to do him out of his natural rights. It was the type specimen of a well-known class of temperament, and produced a personal climate – more unrelieved than most men could sustain – of proud, bitter, contemptuous gloom.

Again typically, this gloom lived side by side with an equally fierce unrealistic optimism. His merits were too great! Some recognition must be on its way! Some blazing fortune was going to arrive!

He was a very strong man physically: at least his bones were heavy and his muscles powerful.[14] That was so of his two sons who survived into maturity (the Trollope genes were more than adequate, all the children were bright, but consumption ran through the family and only Tom and Trollope himself of the children lived past thirty), and was handsome in a stern fashion, which the children were not. He probably had at odd moments a look of defenceless charm, as though appealing for help.

He needed help of the hard-baked businesslike kind, and in Trollope's childhood so did they all. It is not easy to disentangle the practical affairs of the Trollopes. All commentators have relied on the two sources, Tom, writing in his late seventies and a passionate partisan of his mother, and Trollope who at the time of decisive catastrophe was only twelve and too young to understand in detail.

There is a residue of fact. Mr Trollope unquestionably believed that he was heir to his uncle's estate in Hertfordshire. Accordingly the devices of pettier men who were doing him harm at the Bar could be ignored. Actually the uncle's first wife died, and the uncle at the age of sixty promptly married again and fathered six children. There was a family legend that this was entirely due to Mr Trollope refusing, in his obdurate argumentative high-souled manner, not to brandish his liberal principles face to face with the Tory squire. This is the kind of story that families cherish to glorify their misfortunes. Tom believed it all his life.[15] Trollope never refers to it. It seems much more likely that a vigorous man was behaving according to nature.

Similarly there is the fact that Mr Trollope, with Trollope still an infant, lifted the whole family from Keppel Street and, although he kept his chambers in Lincoln's Inn and the pretence of his practice, took up farming. He rented a sizeable amount of land near Harrow on more than sizeable terms and, on this leased land, built a much more than sizeable house.

It was in character for Mr Trollope to assume that, applying the same intellect to farming as he did to Chancery law, he would make a rapid

*Lincoln's Inn Hall. Mr Trollope appeared here in his more
promising days*

success of it. Further, in his sunbursts of optimism he could – for a very
short time, until his uncle made his second marriage – bask in the
thought of his inheritance.

The whole project was carried out with monumental extravagance
and monumental incompetence. The family legend was again that this
was entirely Mr Trollope's doing, the first sign of irreversible decline.
A more detached observer might have some doubts. There is reasonable
suspicion that much of the blame rested on Mrs Trollope.[16]

She was – here there is no doubt at all – the inspiration of the family.
She was a small, pretty, immensely energetic woman. She had indomi-
table guts. Later, when she had to support them all by frenetic writing,
and some of the story became known in literary London, she became a
good deal of a heroine. Dickens much admired her – not as a writer, but
as someone as energetic as himself. Trollope's first biographer admired
her even more.[17]

She loved her husband, to whom she was more than loyal. She loved

[17]

Tom, whom even before Mr Trollope died she made into a surrogate husband. She loved her other children when they were within sight, and otherwise forgot them almost entirely. There was a streak within her of hardness or what we might now call affectiveless. Often, despite her ebullience and outpouringness, her emotions switched off.

Her enemies, and she had some, thought her coarse.[18] That didn't refer to her social origins, or to her conversation (though the Trollopes in general, high Anglicans and proper in their behaviour, were also near enough to the eighteenth century to be less prudish in speech than their more restrained Victorian friends), but probably to this special kind of unfeelingness. Whether that is true or not, she was remarkably thoughtless. In their circumstances – which she must have divined, for she was no fool – she might have thought twice about money. She never did, except, almost literally, until the bailiffs were at the door. She liked living in the state which she thought suitable. Tomorrow something, someone, possibly herself, would provide. There are good arguments for thinking that she was responsible for the scale of Julians, their grand house on the Harrow farm. She went on to be responsible for more and graver follies. More likely than not, there was a resonance between her bouncing euphoria and her husband's self-justifying hopes.

One tincture of excuse. Mr and Mrs Trollope were reckless and incompetent about their money, quite outside the common run: but it is fair to say that so, generally in less dramatic forms, were a good many other of their contemporaries. Perhaps people were a bit bemused by the flow of money, the dazzle of unrestricted capitalism, as they are in countries industrializing themselves today. Anyway, many otherwise sensible persons, up to and beyond the mid nineteenth century, seem not to have understood money at all. Think of Walter Scott. Study the financial adventures in the novels of Dickens, Thackeray, Trollope himself. They are often fatuous to a modern eye, but they were not all imagined. Both Trollope and Dickens were shrewd and prudent about their own affairs, and experienced about those they were depicting.

So the infant Trollope was taken to live on the Harrow farm in an illusion of upper-middle-class prosperity, prosperity so considerable that, if it had been solid, he wouldn't have had to comfort himself in his schooldays that after all he was born a gentleman. In fact, his misery began as soon as he went to school.

2
ODD CHILD OUT

There must have been consolations for the children living on the Harrow farm, though Trollope's autobiography does not admit to them. The boys were vigorous and active, and the two who survived into manhood (Tom and Trollope) enjoyed using their muscles until they were old. Tom was an obsessional long-distance walker all his life (thirty miles a day on holiday was good for the health). For Trollope, hunting and riding were the great minor pleasures of existence.

It was presumably at Julians that he first got astride a horse. Even when Mr Trollope, years later, had to recognize the financial chasm and move to a derelict farmhouse a couple of miles away, they still had prosperous county friends – far more than one would think from Trollope's account. Horses must have been available from early childhood. There is no doubt that he was an adequate, if rough and ready, horseman at an early age.

Mr Trollope still went up to London during the first years of farming at Julians, and so the boys had a certain amount of leisure. When he was present, they hadn't, since Mr Trollope did not believe in leisure. He did believe in education, but his educational strategy and tactics showed his customary bizarre lack of judgment. He drilled Latin grammar into the boys almost as soon as they could talk. Tom and Trollope didn't resist: the middle boy, Henry, his father's favourite, who died young, was a more independent spirit. These lessons were conducted in an atmosphere of gloomy and frantic irritation. He didn't beat them, but as a method of correction pulled their hair.[1] The curious thing is, both Tom and Trollope gained something from this incessant cramming. Mr Trollope was a competent classic in the Wykehamist fashion (his old school, Winchester, was founded by William of Wykeham, hence the name for the pupils) and some of that rubbed off. So did the habit of insensate industry.

Mr Trollope's aim was a simple one. It was to make the boys' educational careers identical with his own. They had to become scholars of

Winchester College Entrance, with the Warden's House, 1816.
'When I was twelve there came the vacancy at Winchester
College which I was destined to fill.' Autobiography

Winchester and Fellows of New College. The first leg, which was fairly easy, duly happened. The second went the way of all Mr Trollope's ambitions, in part through another of his departures from reality.

In the 1820s, and for some time later, a boy became a scholar of Winchester through a complicated process of nomination. There did follow a simple oral examination but it would have taken some ingenuity to be turned down. None of the three Trollope boys was.

Becoming a Fellow of New College was a more formidable undertaking, and required both luck and a good school record.[2] First, it was necessary to be a scholar of Winchester. Second, the number of vacancies varied wildly from year to year as existing Fellows resigned in order to marry or take livings or go to the Bar. This was where the luck came in. Merit also entered. The boys in their final year as Winchester scholars were judged on their past work and put through a distinctly tough oral examination. (Oral examinations sound strange to us, but they are standard practice in Soviet schools and universities to this day.) They were then arranged in order of precedence to fill the New College vacancies. Once at New College they were not scholars in the modern sense, but Fellows from the start, though they were not im-

Harrow, 1816. Note the different classes in the one large hall

mediately taken on to the Foundation, i.e. they didn't receive their two hundred per annum and allowances. There was no further examination or test. More than that, New College retained the right to present its members for degrees without their sitting any university examination.

This probably appears to us as slacker, or more corrupt, than it actually was. It didn't conduce to much first-rate research: but somehow the intellectual level was kept quite high. A closely similar arrangement applied at Cambridge, between Eton and King's, with much the same results. Both carried on until the university reforms of the 1850s.

The Trollope boys took up their scholarships at Winchester at the age of ten, Tom in 1820, Henry in 1821, Trollope in 1825. But before that they were exposed to another of Mr Trollope's brainwaves. It brought Trollope from seven onwards perhaps more suffering than anything else his father did. Even Tom, a good deal less sensitive, remarked on it seventy years later with something like hatred.[3] Mr Trollope sent them all in succession, until their time for Winchester arrived, as day boys to Harrow. In fact, this extraordinary plan appears to have been one of his motives for going near by to live. After all, he could have rented a farm in more suitable places.

Presumably Mr Trollope was proud of this idea of his as a masterly piece of domestic economy. Yet it is hard to think how an intelligent man, even halfway sane, who had himself been to a great English school, could have tolerated it. At this period Harrow was one of the smartest of schools. A fair proportion of the Whig aristocracy sent their sons there. Byron's school friends were nearly all genuine aristocrats. Rich persons, not aristocratic, in pursuit of social cachet, were allured. The average income of Harrovian parents of the 1820s was high. Day boys paid nothing.

England was a rougher country than it is today. Social contempt was openly expressed. Day boys were jeered at as an inferior pauperized breed. The Trollopes were regularly jeered at as they walked up the hill to school. This display of class solidarity (the nearest modern equivalent would be its exact obverse, as if one tried to walk through a picket of strikers) was given an extra edge because the young Trollopes looked so shabby. As another of Mr Trollope's brilliant financial measures (at a time when he was spending hundreds a year on house and farm), the boys seem not to have been provided with any new clothes at all.

The Tea Pot Row at Harrow, or the Battle of Hog Lane, 1825
Inset *Rev. George Butler, head of Harrow 1805–29*

Patches, their sleeves too short, footwear out at heel – it was a sight to arouse moral derision in any right-minded schoolfellow. We mustn't forget that Harrow was an exceptionally opulent school.

Of course, the Trollopes felt wounded, ashamed – and these shames in youth were never quite forgotten. Never quite forgotten and with both Tom and Trollope never quite forgiven. The passages which they wrote about it, as old and successful men, are quiet and discomforting to read.

Winchester, with Trollope now aged ten, was a little better but not much. The social discrimination didn't operate. He came from a Wyke-hamist family, he spoke like a gentleman, brother Tom was getting fairly senior at school. Of course Trollope was frequently beaten, as at Harrow, but nineteenth-century schoolboys took that as the natural condition of man. Since everyone was also frequently beaten, it didn't matter. He had no pocket money, Winchester wasn't so money conscious as Harrow. No, the real trouble was brother Tom. The school had a curious system in which each young boy was given an older boy as 'tutor'. The tutor was supposed to keep an eye on behaviour and academic progress. Tom was appointed to look after Trollope, no doubt as a humane device to ease him in to the school. Tom interpreted his duties rather simply. He thrashed Trollope – so the autobiography says – each day with a large stick.[4]

Trollope remarks temperately that this procedure, passing unnoticed or unchecked, suggests a poor state of supervision at the school. Tom doesn't remark on it at all. Actually, Tom remarks on his brother (dead when Tom was writing, but a great national figure) very little.[5] He does say here and there that Trollope's books had become well known. But, like the rest of the family, he appears to have taken no discernible notice of Trollope in his boyhood. The thrashings were the only sign of life.

Tom and Henry were much of an age, and went on expeditions together. Tom was his mother's favourite by a long stretch, and received loving attention from her. Henry, though a layabout, received as much love as Mr Trollope was capable of giving. Trollope received love from no one, nor even attention. For long periods they seem not to have been aware of his existence. What did they imagine they were doing? It was easier to be the odd child out in a large nineteenth-century family than it would be now. In general, children were not so prized. They were born in large numbers, many died, as with the Trollopes. People accepted the death of children with what to us seems remarkable casualness. But this singular neglect of the young Trollope remains hard to understand. He says little about it, but it stands out bleakly in everything written about the family and in the biographical facts. It may very well have hurt him more than the other miseries of which he did complain.

They seem to have felt that he wasn't much good, or worth taking

The Sick Bed, by Edward Prentis, 1836. '. . . my mother's most visible occupation was that of nursing.' Autobiography

trouble over. That was a classical case of negative judgment, in a family which produced the wisest human judge of the nineteenth century. Great hopes were invested in Tom, who actually had good sound second-rate ability. Considerable efforts, in spite of approaching ruin, were made to find Henry something he wanted to do. No one did that for Trollope. Even when he suddenly broke through and became one of the most famous novelists in England, his mother and Tom scarcely believed it. He still didn't really count.[6]

The most preposterous exhibition of this neglect occurred when he was twelve. Mrs Trollope became friendly with the Wright sisters, who were Scottish-American women of great energy and wealth. They had founded a Utopian settlement and in our time would have been fervent

supporters both of Women's Lib and Black Power. The total amount of
sense possessed by that pair and Mrs Trollope was not large. Among the
three of them they conceived perhaps the scattiest of all Mrs Trollope's
plans.[7] The Trollope family was to remove itself to America and there
Mrs Trollope would restore the family fortunes by opening an emporium
– a kind of primitive general store – in Cincinnati. Between thought and
action with Mrs Trollope there was no discernible gap. The Trollopes, in
instalments, duly went to America. The bazaar was duly opened. Mr
Trollope somehow raised a couple of thousand pounds, and with Tom
followed the rest. As isn't especially surprising, within a couple of years
Mrs Trollope had indomitably lost all the money.

Mrs Trollope's Emporium in Cincinnati. 'I have seen it since . . .
a sorry building! But I have been told that in those days it was
an imposing edifice.' Autobiography

There was one curious feature. As though in a fit of absent-minded-
ness, the young Trollope, in college at Winchester, was left behind. This
still seems taking neglect rather far, even by the standards of the
Trollope family. Trollope did not see his mother for over three years.
There weren't even rudimentary provisions for his holidays. No one was
deputed to look after him. It isn't even clear where he managed to go or
how he managed to feed himself, in what must have been intolerably
long and lonely summer vacations. There was one which he spent, quite
alone, in his father's deserted chambers in Lincoln's Inn. There Trollope
read an old edition of the plays of Shakespeare, because he could find
nothing else to read.

Trollope had a strong nature, as his later life was to prove. But at that

[25]

age, twelve to fifteen, it would have taken a nature impregnably hard not to feel that this loneliness would never end. To add a gothic touch, a lawyer had killed himself in those chambers not long before. Presumably Trollope didn't understand what had brought the family to poverty, nor perhaps how close they were to ruin.[8] But he couldn't help recognizing some of the symptoms. Before Mr Trollope followed his wife, he was by now somewhere near the psychotic edge, possessed by paranoiac fury mixed with speechless gloom – the gloom increased by doses of calomel which were becoming enormous. (Doctors of the period seem to have been remarkably free with their prescriptions. Hence their patients formed these habits. Compare Elizabeth Barrett Browning and Wilkie Collins with their morphine.)[9]

What with Mr Trollope's incapacity and his wife's euphoria, the financial affairs had got lost in confusion, perhaps irreversibly so: though a little earlier, say when Trollope first went to Winchester, a sober prudent head might have rescued a modest living for them.

Anyway, they had let the big house (Julians), it doesn't need saying, without recovering what they still had to pay out – and had moved three miles or so downhill to a little farmhouse called Harrow Weald. Tom paints a slightly more cheerful picture of this place than Trollope; Tom was a more cheerful character and incidentally had more to be cheerful about. He didn't live there much for most of this period, and with mother, sister, brother Henry and father (Mr Trollope is not even mentioned in Tom's account) was having an interesting time in Ohio.

Trollope himself, not mentioned at all in any of the surviving documents, had to live in that farmhouse for long stretches. He says that it was half derelict, the walls – presumably lath and plaster – coming apart, very little furniture, not even bedclothes, food provided by a sulky farm servant and worse than an agricultural labourer's. Much of this can be confirmed from Mrs Trollope's breezy statements later.[10] To put it mildly, it can't have been a comforting place for an adolescent boy on a winter night – or on any other night, as far as that goes.

It might have seemed in existential moments, and would have seemed so when he had developed his nordic stoicism, that since things could hardly be worse, they could in time get better. In fact there must have been moments of the timeless joyous expectations of adolescence, even then, submerged as he was, but the despairs of adolescence are, of course, just as timeless. It's dogged as does it, said some old wiseacre, trying to encourage Mr Crawley in the pit of his troubles.[11] One doubts whether such an exhortation would have been any use to the young Trollope.

Further, though it seemed difficult to imagine, things did get worse. Before he lost all contact, before the catatonic depression which followed rage and persecution mania, Mr Trollope had still managed to mishandle Mrs Trollope's marriage portion. It hadn't been witnessed, and so it wasn't hers. He had also lost trace of the deeds of some London properties. These were the only secure parts of their income, enough to keep them in decent middle-class decorum – in a state rather like Mrs Crawley's lawyer cousin in *The Last Chronicle of Barset*, but with some lofty social connections. Now that had been thrown away, by a kind of wanton or self-destructive carelessness. The comparison with Mr Crawley's behaviour over the twenty-pound cheque is worth noting.

The result of all these disasters on Trollope was cumulative. The family was in America, his school bills at Winchester were not paid, the tradesmen were not allowed to give him credit. He wondered whether he would always be alone, and thought of killing himself. A good many sensitive adolescents – and plenty not so sensitive – have thought of killing themselves. He had more objective cause than most.

Harrow Weald house, by F. Slinger, 1920. 'One of those farm-houses which seem always to be in danger of falling into the neighbourhood horse-pond.' Autobiography. *The house, situated on the northern corner of Weald Lane, was destroyed some time in the 1930s*

[27]

3

WALKING TO SCHOOL

Then things got worse still. Mr Trollope and Tom returned from America in 1830. Trollope was now just over fifteen. Mr Trollope proceeded to exert himself, making almost the last of his decisions. They were as ill-judged as the rest. There was even less excuse for them, for he had been through all the English academic hoops and should have been on his home ground.

The fact was, losing hundreds of pounds a year, running into bankruptcy, he was obsessed with saving every shilling on his children. But the saving was tiny, and the loss out of proportion.

Since Tom couldn't get his Fellowship at New College, he was sent to Oxford, not to a college, but to a tiny residential hall.[1] That effectively quashed Tom's chances, until he became his mother's escort and finally settled with her in Florence. Then, in circumstances not yet completely explained, he lived a life of expatriate prosperity.

As for Trollope, Mr Trollope did the incredible. The incredible, that is, if he had been aware of his son's feelings. Probably he wasn't aware of any feelings other than his own. He took Trollope away from Winchester, and sent him back to Harrow as a day boy.

Even on the practical level, this was a fatuous choice. Characteristically it destroyed the last chance, and a good chance, of Mr Trollope's own lifelong ambition. He had been right through the process himself, and should have known the odds as well as any man. It was a simple calculation. A Winchester scholar's likelihood of getting a Fellowship at New College depended (a) on the number of vacancies falling open in New College, and (b) on the competition in his own year of entry – his 'election' as the term was – in the school. Tom happened to belong to a particularly good election, with half a dozen contenders demonstrably better academics than he was. Thus, unless Fellows of New College suddenly married in droves, his chances were slim. Whereas Trollope belonged to a poor election, with only a couple of clever boys. He was himself not an academic flyer, but by no means bad, despite his own propaganda to the contrary, echoed by others. He would have been adequate enough in the sixth form at Winchester.[2] The odds were heavily on his becoming a Fellow of New College at the age of nineteen.

What would have happened if he had? As a rule sheer luck plays a bigger part than we like to think, in a life as much an obstacle race as Trollope's. But for once the answer is pretty obvious. He would have become a clergyman. In his time Oxford, and Cambridge also, were not universities in our sense at all, but liberal arts colleges attached to the Church of England. A high proportion of their graduates, over sixty per cent, duly became priests of the Church of England. For Trollope, there would be no conceivable reason against that for himself. He didn't approve of 'enthusiasm' in religion, but as a young man he was a steady High Anglican. He wouldn't have fallen for the Oxford Movement, any more than Archdeacon Grantly did: but like Archdeacon Grantly he would have harked back to the days of good sense and true religion, when a bishop enjoyed playing cards in his own palace.

Trollope would, of course, have seen some worldly advantages in becoming an Anglican priest. He would have been the last man, almost literally the last man, to pretend otherwise: and he was not fond of men who did so pretend or who wouldn't use any introspective insight. He couldn't have avoided getting a decent living, either through New College or his family connections. He was an able man, quite separately from his deepest gifts, and the qualities which brought him moderate success in the Post Office would have brought him similar success in the Church.

He probably would have quarrelled with too many superiors to become a bishop. Further, he was a Whig, and his churchmanship wouldn't have made him a comfortable Whig bishop.[3] But it is quite easy to imagine him as an immensely energetic, rough and ready, perceptive archdeacon. Instead of writing about the clerical life, he would have lived it. He would certainly have written books too, for he was a born writer. It is hard to guess what they would have been like, except they certainly wouldn't have been novels whose main characters were Anglican clergymen.

Mr Trollope extinguished that agreeable prospect. Instead, back at Harrow, Trollope was plunged into more misery. Once more the old patched clothes, the shabbiest boy in the fashionable school. Like his brother Tom at the same age – Tom was otherwise not a specially vulnerable boy or man, but with both it was a thorn in the flesh – he worried about being physically displeasing. 'I was big and awkward and ugly, and, I have no doubt, skulked about in a most unattractive manner. Of course I was ill-dressed and dirty.'[4]

That was written about Winchester, but the wound was even more

[29]

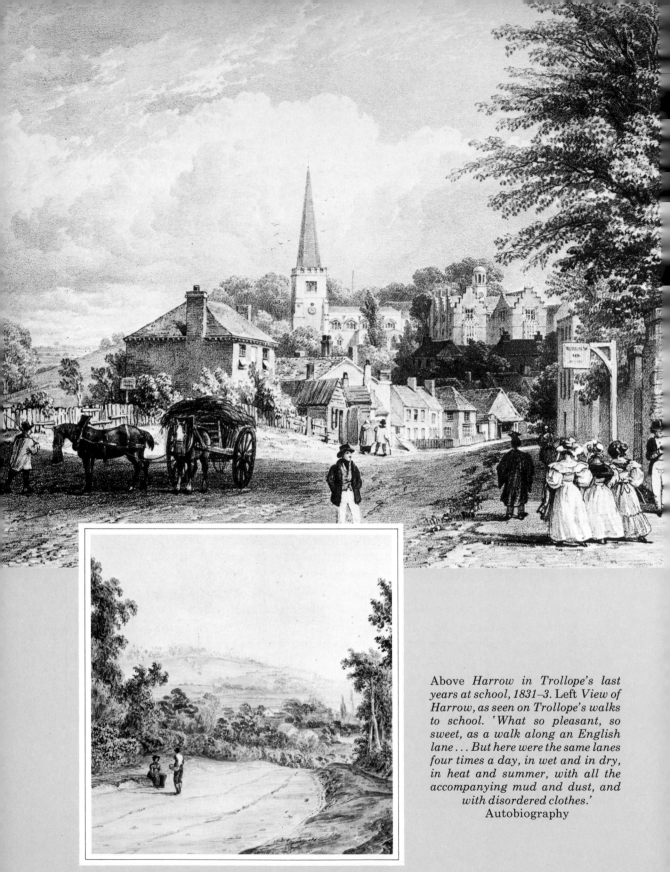

Above *Harrow in Trollope's last years at school, 1831–3.* Left *View of Harrow, as seen on Trollope's walks to school.* 'What so pleasant, so sweet, as a walk along an English lane ... But here were the same lanes four times a day, in wet and in dry, in heat and summer, with all the accompanying mud and dust, and with disordered clothes.'
Autobiography

mordant in that desolate period at Harrow. The long walks[5] each way through the country lanes, alternately muddy or dirty, made him dirtier still. His pride was savaged. He says that he had no friends. His contemporaries didn't hide their scorn for a charity boy. As a matter of cold, historical fact, he was on good terms later with some of those contemporaries, who knew him as a famous man. They left no reminiscences of him as a schoolboy. There is just one record, and it adds some colour to the bitter picture. It was written after Trollope's autobiography had been published, and may have been influenced by it. Some of it, as we now know, is inaccurate, but it comes from a lively and good-natured man.

> I avoided him, for he was rude and uncouth, but I thought him an honest brave fellow. His faults were external; all the rest of him was right enough. But the faults were of that character for which schoolboys will never make allowances and so poor Trollope was tabooed ... He gave no sign of promise whatever, was always in the lowest part of the form ...[6]

That is a passage from the memoirs of Sir William Gregory of Coole, produced in old age. He was a cheerful and clever Anglo-Irish squire, a competent member of the Ascendancy, who flourished in London society and Westminster, and finished as Governor of Ceylon.[7]

Only a few years after those Harrow days, Trollope was a frequent guest at Coole, and the two of them rode hard to hounds together. Very much later, when they were in their sixties, Trollope stayed for weeks with him in the governor's mansion in Ceylon.

Some of Gregory's reminiscences may be derived from the amiable human impulse to recall eminent men in their youth as being more derelict than they really were. Trollope admits in the autobiography that he finished as seventh boy in the school and a monitor. He says he never won a prize. That was a slip of memory. It has been discovered that, to the credit of some unknown Harrow master, he won an English essay prize.[8] Nevertheless the general impression in Gregory's memory was close to Trollope's own, and must contain something of the truth.

Gregory as an aging widower married the woman who became the benefactor of Yeats and the Abbey Theatre. In the middle 1960s, Frank O'Connor – who understood Trollope's art better than most men and wrote about it admirably – used to talk about Lady Gregory and of how she told him of her husband's connection with Trollope. That went back over one hundred and thirty years, and was a pleasant example of literary continuity.[9]

In the autobiography, Trollope himself did not choose to select, or simply forgot, any sign of improved academic performance. The solitary triumph he was proud of at Harrow was a fight. Some boy had baited him once too often. Trollope was abnormally touchy even when an elder statesman and outwardly harmonious: much more so as a boy, when he had good reason to be. He was also a fighting man. His tormentor had to be sent home and did not re-appear for a number of days.

For Trollope, Harrow meant, and continued to mean, those walks through the country lanes into humiliation. Nothing but that. Humiliations cut deeper than griefs. Yet, in those walks, he escaped into a habit, which almost certainly began earlier, of constructing his own kind of daydream. These were daydreams in the shape of stories, with himself as the main character, but more realistic, or at least less impossible, than most daydreams. This was a habit which was to serve him well. He had a knack of keeping these stories, and the other people in them as well as himself, continually in his mind.[10]

The other people in them, one can guess, were usually drawn from those he knew. Perhaps they were giving him affection, but in a fashion which might just happen. With his special obsessive interest in people, the same personages in the stories were likely to be taken up day after day. It is conceivable that the story of Johnny Eames (in the shape of Trollope) rescuing Lord De Guest from the bull had its first origins in some of those walks to the detested school.

Actually, practical matters brightened up for the Trollope family through a fairy story such as Trollope wouldn't have allowed himself to invent. Mrs Trollope, at last returning from America, took on the role of benevolent wizard. She hadn't hurried back to her husband and Trollope. Entirely undeterred, or apparently unaffected, by the financial catastrophe in Cincinnati, she had spent an enjoyable year trapesing round the eastern seaboard.[11]

The males of her family (the second son very ill, Mr Trollope ill and increasingly demented) were out of sight in England and for effective purposes out of mind. Mrs Trollope was enraptured by the sight of New York from the Hudson – New York, then only the battery and lower Manhattan, was one of the most beautiful towns on earth, and Mrs Trollope's visual taste was excellent.

During that year of sightseeing she had been writing down her impressions of America. Then these, called *Domestic Manners of the Americans*, with the speed of early nineteenth-century publication, were duly produced soon after she came back to Harrow Weald, and – transformation scene – the family suddenly had an illusion of being well off again. The farmhouse was made comfortable.[12]

Opposite *Vista View of Harrow, from the east side of the park, by W. Cowen, 1845. Too well known to the youthful Trollope for too long*

Trollope soon had a pillow for his head, and may have been given a new suit. With characteristic extravagance, Mrs Trollope shortly acquired yet another house, higher up the hill, so his way to school was shorter and perhaps less dolorous. This house was quite near to the first great one, Julians, which had been the beginning of their ruin.[13]

Mrs Trollope, perhaps the least superstitious or wood-touching woman who ever lived, christened the new house Julians Hill: just as after one daughter called Emily had died of TB in infancy, Mrs Trollope gave the same name to her youngest daughter.[14]

All these arrangements Mrs Trollope made entirely by herself. Mr Trollope now went unnoticed, relapsed into psychotic despair, and also sickening, though what the disease was remains mysterious. He wasn't yet sixty, but he had become an old man. After Mrs Trollope's literary success, he had applied himself, hour after hour, day after day, to literary work of his own. It was the kind of gigantesque enterprise that unsuccessful writers sometimes apply themselves to, so as to see no conceivable end. It was nothing less than an Ecclesiastical Encyclopedia, that is an encyclopedia of all ecclesiastical terms that had ever existed. When he died, he had got as far as letter D. As he worked, only Trollope could see some pathos there.

Mrs Trollope hadn't really made a fortune out of *Domestic Manners of the Americans*, only nine hundred pounds in the first year. She seems never to have written before, but she had more natural fluency than any other member of the family, which is saying a remarkable amount. She was also a good observer of anything in front of her eyes – she had no sense of the future and no historical insight. Nevertheless, the book still reads fresh, snobbish, malicious, irrepressible, often funny, curiously enough more sympathetic than the total flavour of her personality. It has something of the impact of Malcolm Muggeridge writing about the Soviet Union.[15] In modern times, she would have been a first-rate descriptive journalist. None of that endeared her to Americans of the 1830s.

None of that, also, delayed the Trollopes' bankruptcy more than a couple of years. Mrs Trollope was the only money-earner in the family. Indomitably she wrote a couple of novels, another travel book, and then started another novel. She spent the trickle of money (she didn't repeat her first success) as fast as she earned it. A little of her own inheritance had been – through the devotion, totally unpaid, of a relation's solicitor[16] – secured to her. That, plus the literary earnings, added up to about two

Opposite *Mrs Frances Trollope, 1832, by Auguste Hervieu, friend and supporter of Mrs Trollope and illustrator of several of the Trollopes' books*

*Julians Hill, the original of Orley Farm, by Sir John Everett
Millais*

hundred and fifty a year for them all. Tom, whom she was grooming as a
kind of support or social husband, might now earn a living for himself.
She even gave one of her infrequent thoughts to Trollope. It was on the
fringe of possibility that he might earn a living for himself too. Meanwhile she would transport the whole brood to Bruges, where living would
be cheap.

This duly happened: but as before with the Trollopes in a climate of
black farce. All the accumulated Harrow debts, Julians, Julians Hill, the
farmhouse, the land, the tradesmen, were piling up on Mr Trollope. She
suddenly realized, as a more apprehensive woman would have done
months before, that unless he was removed to safety where the law
couldn't touch him, he would find himself in the Marshalsea. (This was
1834, with imprisonment for debt in active operation.)

So he was lifted out of England, apathetic and ill, with a few hours to
spare. Somehow Mrs Trollope must have had a private warning. For

*Quarter Day: the Discomforts of Moving. The Trollopes had
many such*

once Trollope, who had just left Harrow, was put to use. Early one morning he was commanded to drive his father in the gig to London Docks.
Trollope hadn't the faintest idea what was happening or why his father
asked to be taken to the Ostend boat. Trollope's mystification shows how
far he had been shut out of his mother's confidence. Even so it does seem
peculiarly obtuse, for someone who was to become so sharp-eyed.

He did learn what was happening, on his drive home to Julians Hill.
Someone told him that the bailiffs were in. The whole scene, with friendly
neighbours helping to secrete favourite objects from the house, appears
to have been regarded by all as a farce, but not a black one. Trollope had
many shames and miseries in his youth, but he took bailiffs and debts
with a reasonable approach to early nineteenth-century casualness. He
didn't feel any of the tormented mortification from which, after not dis-
similar events, Dickens was never quite healed.

In instalments the family settled themselves in a large bleak house at

[35]

Bruges. By now, though, the farce had evanesced. Three of them were mortally sick, Mr Trollope, the second son Henry now aged twenty-three, and Emily (the second daughter given that name) aged fifteen. Whether Mr Trollope knew he was near his death is not clear. Henry probably didn't know about his own. Mrs Trollope knew about both of them.

Bruges

4

OCCUPATION FOR A
YOUNG MAN

Only a women of Mrs Trollope's toughness could have survived the next twenty months in the house at Bruges. Her husband was dying as he had lived, sometimes in schizoid stupor, sometimes in fits of demanding rage, dragging himself to work on the Ecclesiastical Encyclopedia. Henry, as his lungs rotted, became as ill tempered and importunate as his father. He showed none of the sweetness of some consumptives in the terminal stages, but a good deal of a consumptive's hope.

If his mother wasn't so careful with her money, there must be a cure – he shouted for her angrily night and day. When she had finally got them both to sleep, she had to keep herself awake and write two or three thousand words of her new novel. Otherwise, within a few months, she wouldn't be able to buy the food. Emily the second was a gentle girl, much loved by Trollope, and gave no trouble. She, too, was infected. It was a household fit for Ibsen.[1]

Tom, Mrs Trollope's one spiritual support, had gone off to earn his keep as a private tutor in London, so as to lessen her expenses. As usual brisk and competent in the short term (and managing to stay singularly cheerful), she decided it was time that Trollope too should get out of the house. That she contrived, but her first idea was one of her most hare-brained. By some means which have not been revealed, she procured for him an offer of a commission in the Austrian cavalry. The minor fact that he knew no German, and very little French, did not deter her or her source of influence. Trollope was to be allowed a year's grace to learn the languages. Mrs Trollope's method of achieving this was to get him appointed as a classics master in a school teaching English boys in Brussels.[2]

Then she had another idea, not so bizarre, and used a more reasonable source of influence, so that at the age of nineteen Trollope was also in London, with a job in the Post Office.[3]

At the end of that year 1834, Henry died his lingering death. Tom was summoned to the funeral, as the quasi-husband he was to be for the rest

Left *Girl Writing by Lamplight, by William Henry Hunt. While in Bruges, Mrs Trollope had to keep herself awake at night to write her new novel, otherwise, within a few months she wouldn't have been able to buy food for the family.* Right *Illustration from Mrs Trollope's* Paris and the Parisians, *by Auguste Hervieu. After Tom and Anthony had started work in England Mrs Trollope was financed in a trip to Paris by her publisher. She attended many soirées like this, as, in fact, did Trollope when he came over to see her in 1839*

of Mrs Trollope's life. Trollope was not summoned. Two months later Mr Trollope died. He was buried near to Henry in the Protestant cemetery at Bruges. Again Tom was called for. Again Trollope wasn't.

No wonder, he cried out in old age that, at nineteen, he often cursed the hour he had been born.[4] Even in his sixties that wretchedness was unassuaged. That will be mentioned later. Of himself at nineteen, though, he wrote: 'I acknowledge the weakness of a great desire to be loved – of a strong wish to be popular with my associates. No child, no boy, no lad, no young man, had ever been less so.' Call that self-pity, if you like, if you are certain that from identical experience you would have been immune from self-pity yourself.[5]

[38]

At nineteen he was starting his life in London. He was utterly on his own. He had no conception what to do with himself: though half unknown to his own mind resolutions were forming in that deep interior. All our information about him at this period, and for several years afterwards, comes from his own writing, explicit in his autobiography and truthful in terms of fact, implicit and more truthful, because art is truer than any factual record, in two novels. Charlie Tudor in *The Three Clerks* tells us something about Trollope's young life, but only on the surface. John Eames in *The Small House at Allington* and *The Last Chronicle of Barset* tells us much more.

Eames is a real self-portrait, the only one he ever did. It is a little decorated, and in one or two places romanticized, as self-portraits usually are, but it carries the bite of experience. Not even a writer as inventive as Trollope at his peak could have invented that.[6]

Anyway, those half-disclosures are all we have, literally all, of Trollope between the ages of nineteen and twenty-six. There are no reminiscences of him anywhere, not even gossip or oral tradition. There are half a dozen letters of his own, all but one (a description to Tom of Emily's death) formal. Any additions or anecdotes come only from himself in later life, told to men (such as Escott, his first biographer, or Edmund Yates, a peculiarly unreliable channel) many years younger.

One can guess, however, what young Trollope looked like. He is fond of using the word hobbledehoy, impartially about himself or Johnny Eames. He was a lumbering young man, strong, powerfully muscled. Later in life he put on weight and acquired physical presence. His physique, like his personality, was more complex than it seemed, finer nerved, less of a piece. He had small hands and feet and danced very well. It was the kind of physical temperament made to endure, as he would have been the first to observe in another. He was as interested as all good novelists in the relation between psyche and soma.

People always thought him very large. By late twentieth-century standards, this might not strike us. The average and median height have gone up inches since his time. He was probably about five feet ten. We know exactly how tall his brother Tom was, since he tells us – five feet eight, and he was considered big.[7] Trollope was unusually conscious of being physically unpleasing. He had no vanity, and could have done with more – unlike Dickens who had physical charm and knew it. Trollope didn't like looking at himself in mirrors, or being photographed.

His features were undistinguished and set down in no particular order. As an older man, given a large beard, brown hair turning white early, he became agreeably impressive in a patriarchal fashion. The only noticeable feature about his face in youth would have been his eyes – dark blue, so pigmented that some thought them black, behind his spectacles constantly observant, penetrating, on the watch. All his life they were re-marked on. W. H. Sheldon would have drawn psychosomatic conclusions from such eyes.[8] They were not in harmony with the lumpish aspects of his body.

As well as having no confidence that his appearance was pleasing, Trollope had no sexual confidence. In some young men the two things need not run together, but they stand out painfully in all that he wrote about himself and Eames. His young manhood was more anxious in consequence, though curiously he probably gained as a writer. His insight into young women, as delicate and searching as any novelist's, wouldn't have been given to a man, say Maupassant or Gorky, without the faintest element of sexual diffidence.

In his youth Trollope was, and remained all his life, intensely 'susceptible' – to use a word he was fond of applying to Johnny Eames and which was still popular among the feminine confidences of well brought up young women a century later. He loved the company of women, liked flirtations and the half-prospect of marriage (think of Eames' absurd adventures elsewhere when obsessively in love with Lily Dale).

He enjoyed like Stendhal all the preliminary minuets of love. He went on constructing his daydream stories, never quite impossible, often worked out as realistically as his written stories were to be, with himself as the main character and attractive young women surprisingly drawn to him. All of these results of his susceptibility were to be valuable to the future novelist. They didn't take away the frustration of his London years, and one feels that he can't have had much fun.

At nineteen he still had to build a character. He was extraordinarily passive, in the light of what he became. He accepted his mother's instructions, either to join the Austrian army or the Post Office, with a kind of dumb obedience. He seems to have had no vocational direction whatever (there is just one latent indication to the contrary). He had no idea how he was to earn a living,or, in his own favourite phrase, earn his bread.

This may have been partly due to his lonely loveless childhood. It was certainly also due to the eccentricities of nineteenth-century English upper-class education. Trollope had been at two major schools from the age of seven to nineteen. During that time he had learned nothing, precisely nothing, except Latin and Greek. He says that he didn't even know those well, though that could have been his own fault, or the result of his miseries.[9]

He had been taught no modern language and he never spoke one with any ease. (Tom spent many years in Italy, and didn't become adequate in Italian. They must have been poor natural linguists, though Mrs Trollope was a good one. So was Dickens.) He knew no science. He hadn't learned elementary arithmetic. He had to acquire his multiplication tables when

Sir Francis Freeling, secretary to the Post Office 1797–1836,
through whom Trollope obtained his position in the Post Office

he was a government official. Incidentally he shows signs here and there of acquiring them shakily. He was better read than most boys of his age in English literature and history, but only because he had been so much deserted at home and books were his one solace.

It was a bizarre education. One gets the same story from many of his contemporaries.[10] The aim of the most privileged English education (Rugby under Arnold got away from it a little) was to enable bright boys to write Latin and Greek composition in prose and verse – and the brightest products of the system wrote better classical pastiche than anyone in Europe. At school, they did this all the time, and went on doing it until quite recently. European scholars thought, as they have done since, that the English were slightly mad. To be so easy in Latin, was an enviable facility, no doubt. But to spend one's entire education upon it ... It had given Porson and Housman an unsurpassable textual taste. Even there, only a freak could employ it for serious scholarship, and in nineteenth-century classical scholarship the Germans, more sensibly trained, had beaten the English out of the field.[11]

Perhaps it is no wonder that Trollope acquiesced to any of his mother's brainwaves. The Austrian cavalry, the Post Office, they seemed much of a muchness. So he became a junior civil servant at ninety pounds a year. Which, of course, determined the whole of his official life.

He passed those first years at the Post Office, according to his own account, as an idle graceless 'hobbledehoy', living in squalid lodgings in Marylebone, employed on work so mechanical that it would have seemed intolerable to a less depressed young man. All that rings true, but one ought to notice the first of the handful of his youthful letters that have survived. When he wrote it, he was not yet twenty. He was addressing the publisher Richard Bentley on a piece of his mother's business.[12] This he does in a competent manner, and with no sort of diffidence. He doesn't sound a bit like a hobbledehoy, but as though he was used to coping with successful men on something like even terms. The same applies to letters a couple of years later, to John Murray and again to Bentley, also written on his mother's behalf. It brings back the thought that Johnny Eames sometimes forgets his humiliation, is capable of being easy in good company, and behaves like an authoritative young man.

More revealing is the final paragraph in that first letter to Bentley.

> I now ask to trouble you on my own less important score – Is it in your power to lend me any assistance in procuring the insertion of lucubrations of my own in any of the numerous periodical magazines etc. which come out in such monthly swarms – I am not aware whether you are yourself the Proprietor of any such – my object of course is that of turning my time to any account that I am able ...

Creative writers don't suddenly spring up out of nothing. Trollope himself says that there wasn't a day in those years when he didn't think of writing novels, but wrote none. That has to be accepted as it were as the legal truth. It is however difficult to think that he didn't sometimes put down words on paper.

5

SURVIVAL IN THE PUBLIC SERVICE

To enter the Civil Service in Trollope's time, and for a generation after, a young man had to be nominated. Mrs Trollope knew a great many people, through birth, literary success and her reputation for heroism in her catastrophe, and she remembered one such sympathizer who happened to be the wife of a senior Post Office official. This official was the son of Sir Francis Freeling, the Post Office chief.[1] Hence a nomination for Trollope.

Until he died Trollope much approved of this method of recruitment. In his habitual modesty he couldn't see how else he could ever have been a public servant. Impoverished gentlemen like himself had standards of responsibility and honour that made valuable public servants. He himself ultimately turned out, in an eccentric fashion, a very good one. Unlike Carlyle and his later intellectual friends, he couldn't get reconciled to the Northcote-Trevelyan reforms. Appointments by competitive examination or merit appalled him[2] – though he forgave Charles Trevelyan for his evil reforms when they were both old men.

In fact, there was a slightly comic pretence of an examination for the young man nominated. (For Treasury candidates, this was more than a pretence, and Trollope couldn't have got in.) The account of Charlie Tudor's examination in *The Three Clerks* can be taken as strictly accurate. We know comparatively little of the working of the pre-Trevelyan Civil Service from the inside,[3] and Trollope is a primary source. Tudor (i.e. Trollope) goes to St Martin's-le-Grand with his sponsor (in real life the younger Freeling, husband of Mrs Trollope's friend), is interviewed by his sponsor's brother who is a more senior official. He is asked to give a specimen of handwriting. In his nervousness he covers the page with blots (as the young Trollope seems to have been always capable of doing). It is kindly suggested that he go away and try to make a fair copy by himself. Can he do arithmetic? This is horrifying. A little, he says. They will test him on the rule of three tomorrow.

Tomorrow, though, they have decided to forget the fair copy and the arithmetic, and he is installed as a Post Office clerk. Clerk meant nothing derogatory. It was the nineteenth-century term for a civil servant, and lasted in the Foreign Office down to the Second World War – which caused misunderstanding among foreigners, who thought that being sent a chief clerk was an insult.

Though the term clerk is misleading, most of Trollope's work, as with that of any young man in the Secretary's office, was miserably clerical. They spent a lot of time copying out letters by hand – by hand, because there were no means of mechanical reproduction (it is easy to forget how these have transformed office business), and because the Civil Service hadn't yet equipped itself with massive populations of subsidiary grades. Johnny Eames is allowed to draft letters for the Secretary, which he does a good deal better than the Secretary could himself: but that is after he has been befriended by lofty persons. Trollope may have had a few such opportunities for official composition, but not many. There is little evidence, in fact, that in seven years at St Martin's-le-Grand he

Left *The General Post Office, Inland Office, 1841*. Right *The Mail Arriving at Temple Bar, 1834*

was ever given a job which would have vaguely interested a sentient human being. He was the last young man – unlike the more compliant and boss-pleasing Yates, who entered thirteen years later into the same office – to manufacture interest for himself.

Yet it is facile to be unfair to the Civil Service of this period. They were groping their way into an entirely different administrative world. Their structures emerged from the eighteenth century, for which even then they were barely adequate, and had to fit themselves for a society needing to be far more articulated, to an extent which no one alive then completely understood. In some respects, the country was having to create what is now called an infrastructure, rather as a rich developing country like Nigeria is having to do today – railways, communications, public services, the matrix of a modern state. The Civil Service, starting from a simpler and more traditional base, had to get involved in much of this. They did it pretty well. Some of the top civil servants were as clever and as dutiful as any since. Men like Trevelyan, the Stephens, Cardwell, would have been heads of the Treasury, Permanent Secretaries of Departments, in our own time.

There is one interesting feature about them, compared with their successors. Since the society was administratively primitive, in an unorganized state of development, they had to get nearer the actual level of operations. Their work was not as abstract. They had to perform more like the initiators of great businesses – like Henry Ford i rather than Henry Ford ii. The very best administrator in nineteenth-century England, better than those just mentioned, was Florence Nightingale. She appointed herself something like an additional Permanent Secretary to the War Office. She had to discover for herself what nursing was like. Nowadays she could have done that by reading papers.

To get them all into perspective, it is necessary to forget about the Circumlocution Office.[4] On these matters, unlike some others, Dickens had no more knowledge and insight than a modern satirical journalist, letting fly at the Circumlocution Office's descendants. There were, it is true, delectable oddities about Trollope's Civil Service not possible among the descendants. One example was Sir Henry Taylor.

Sir Henry Taylor was, in nineteenth-century intellectual England, one of the venerated figures. He was a man of handsome stately appearance and benevolent personality. He was a good civil servant who, though he wouldn't accept the top position, occupied a high place at the Colonial Office for nearly half a century. What would surprise many people as they think of the imperialist fervour at its apogee, Taylor and his chief colleagues were temperately liberal minded (sometimes, of course, paternally so) in their views of colonial administration. They hadn't much influence on the imperialist fervour, but at least they tried

[45]

to civilize it. Taylor wrote, in beautifully lucid English, many enlightened minutes.

Like most of the Civil Service characters in Trollope's novels, Taylor came from a moderately genteel family. His father was a younger son of a Cumberland squire. This was usually the case with Victorian high civil servants – in life as in fiction. They were the sons of parsons, squires, doctors, the sub-class Trollope knew so well. They weren't aristocrats, nothing like the Barnacles. Dickens got all that quite wrong. They were the beginning of a *haute bourgeoisie* which became important in English life for a hundred and fifty years.

Taylor entered the Colonial Office in 1824[5] and was still drawing his full official salary until the age of seventy-two. (He died at eighty-six, and his pension was nearly equal to that full salary.) That wouldn't happen nowadays. And it wouldn't happen nowadays that there was a special reason why he was so universally admired. It wasn't that he was a good and clever civil servant or that he was charming, benign and good-looking. No doubt that helped: but the chief reason was that he wrote verse dramas.

A large number of Victorian intellectuals wrote verse dramas. They were usually execrable. They were not often put on the stage. When they were, they flopped. Even if they didn't flop, the financial rewards were tiny. Play-writing wasn't a profitable occupation in the nineteenth century. Nevertheless, writing verse dramas seems to have been regarded as one of the chief aspirations of man. Sir Henry Taylor's were no worse than most others. His best were probably better than Tennyson's, which were about as bad as a man of literary genius could produce. In Taylor's best-known work, *Philip van Artevelde*, there are some scenes, and quite a lot of lines, which are still worth looking at.[6]

Among his contemporaries he had an enormous reputation. The play was published, and they all read it. Trollope frequently used quotations from the play in his text and in chapter headings. After many years it did at last reach the theatre, and duly flopped. That didn't matter. Verse dramas had only a vestigial connection with the stage. *Philip van Artevelde* gave Sir Henry Taylor his sacrosanct place not only in literary society, but in society as a whole.

In the early seventies there was a determined effort, which nearly succeeded, to introduce life peerages, already in existence for Law Lords. A good many eminent Victorians, for a variety of reasons, some financial, didn't wish to accept hereditary peerages, but would have been pleased to sit in the Upper House. A list of potential life peers was drawn

Opposite *Sir Henry Taylor in his mid-sixties. Photograph by
Julia Margaret Cameron*

[47]

up, between twenty and thirty. It was a reputable list, including some distinguished names, and number two on the list was the inevitable Sir Henry Taylor.

It was considered fitting and proper that he should want plenty of time for thought and artistic creation. No one objected when he decided to remove his household to Sheen, at a safe distance from Whitehall, so that he would be spared the day-to-day trivial business of the office. Despatch boxes were transported to Sheen. He continued to write enlightened minutes. He ceased to attend the office. After a time, however, he felt that Sheen was rather too near the heart of things to be completely satisfactory for purposes of reflection. So he removed himself further, this time to Bournemouth, now in his sixties, still number three at the Colonial Office, still writing enlightened minutes, there to pass, serene, undistracted by Whitehall commotion, loved and venerated, the last dozen years of his career.

It is fair to say that that couldn't happen nowadays. Trollope extracted some amusement out of absentee canons, but he never directed any attention to absentee civil servants. Perhaps, when Sir Henry Taylor's stately progress was beginning, Trollope was in no condition to be amused. Yet Taylor, who was a friend of Mrs Trollope (they met and enjoyed themselves at the court of Louis Philippe, both capable of getting on anywhere), would have befriended Trollope, if he had been allowed. At least Taylor said so in old age, having outlived Trollope, a dozen years his junior, and read his autobiography. There is no reason to doubt this. Taylor was one of the kindest of men and was surrounded by adoring young women, who would have been good for Trollope.

If you were Sir Henry Taylor you knew how pleasant a civil servant's life could be. It looked somewhat different from lower down.

Opposite *The Royal Mails Starting from the General Post Office* (detail), *by James Pollard, 1830*

6

THE BEST YEARS OF
ONE'S LIFE?

In those years Trollope wasn't in a mood to be befriended by Sir Henry Taylor, or men older than Sir Henry Taylor. He hated his job, the office, his superiors. Except for slices of luck, the job was routine. How anyone could be either good or bad at it, or display any aptitude for higher things, remains baffling. Possibly by looking efficient, keeping punctual office hours (which weren't exacting, 10 am to 4.30 pm), being polite to superiors and not attracting unfavourable notice.

According to his own account, Trollope couldn't manage any of those things. It is hard to judge how unsatisfactory he was, or whether he was, as he says, constantly on the edge of being sacked.[1] Certainly all through his official career he was abnormally incompetent at getting on with superiors. His pride, and the façade of personality that he was building, were too much for him. He was inept at bringing out the emollient word – very odd for a man whose fiction is full of the subtlest of emollient words.

Certainly also, he was full of the rancour of an ambitious young man who knows he has powers, is savage because they aren't being used, feels that the months, the years, are being gnawed away. He sees his contemporaries rising when he has done nothing. There were times in the long, communal, noisy, liquor-smelling office in St Martin's-le-Grand when Victorians would have said that he was eating his heart out.

It isn't surprising that at twenty-four he had an illness, so serious that people wondered if he would survive, but which wasn't properly diagnosed.[2] That has happened often enough to young men under his kind of strain. His physique, though, was powerful enough to conquer greater strain than that: and so, fighting against his native depression, was his appetite for life.

We don't know what consolations he found outside the office, or whether there were many, or how he spent his time. There must have

Opposite *The General Post Office, One Minute to Six* (detail),
by G. E. Hicks, 1860

[49]

Belgrave Square, which Lady Holland called 'that swamp'

been diversions. Even Trollope concedes, shamefacedly, that there were happy moments. He went at weekends on gigantic walks with a couple of friends. They were hearty youths, enjoying their own strength and making themselves tired.[3] And they were lit up by the limitless hopes of youth. Trollope must have dreamed – he hadn't left off his realistic day-dreams – of the day when he would become a famous writer.

They had cheerful times, too, in the pubs. London was still a rough town in this decade and later. Most of the upper-class residential districts were already built, and the great squares were handsome. Cubitt was just beginning work on his great development, turning the marshy kitchen gardens south of Knightsbridge into the seemliest bit of domestic urban planning in Europe (Lady Holland, however, refused to live in 'that swamp', meaning Belgrave Square). Nevertheless, there were plenty of menacing slums. St Giles and Seven Dials still existed. An able-bodied man, if he was prudent, took care where he walked at night, even in the middle of London. The pubs and eating-houses would seem to us as harsh and noisy as those of a frontier town.

[50]

Left *The Barmaid, by Paul Gavarni.* Right *The Publican's
Tale* (detail), *by Robert Walker Macbeth*

Both Edmund Yates, not a fastidious man, and Tom Trollope commented on how coarse the material life in London really was, and by
comparison how civilized the 1850s had become. Trollope carefully up-
dated the conditions of Johnny Eames from those of his own time as a
Post Office clerk. We have to imagine Trollope living in ramshackle
lodgings in Marylebone (the street has disappeared), not often getting a
decent meal, constantly in debt for small amounts, since ninety pounds
per annum didn't go far even then, helped out spasmodically by his
mother.[4] There was plenty of drinking – usually gin or brandy – with his
fellow clerks, in dark, sleezy pubs. They would often be uproarious, the
drink and sleezy pubs were no doubt exhilarating to healthy twenty-
year-olds – and Trollope, like other men with a depressive streak, had a
fund of high spirits in company. There would be some clumsy flirting
with the girls who served them.

There may also have been slightly more audacious flirting with land-
ladies' daughters and similar young women. This plays a largish part in
Eames's London life,[5] and he doesn't behave with much sensitivity.

[51]

Trollope tells us that a woman invaded the Post Office one day and asked him loudly when he was going to marry her daughter. He adds that he was as innocent as a man could reasonably be.[6] This we must accept. If he had been guilty, and above all if he had seduced a girl, he would have been the first to accuse himself – and to take more blame than he deserved. The overwhelming probability is that none of these flirtations led to anything, but that girls less diffident than he was may have been taken in by the elaborate flirtatious half-promising manoeuvres of a diffident man.

Yet he says, with great emphasis, that his life was sordid. 'There was no house in which I could habitually see a lady's face and hear a lady's voice. No allurement to decent respectability came in my way. It seems to me that in such circumstances the temptations of life would almost certainly prevail with a young man . . . the temptations at any rate prevailed with me.'[7]

What did he mean? Michael Sadleir decided – on no firmer evidence than any of us have – that he meant very little, just a lot of drinking, a bit of roistering through the streets, no more.[8] In historical fact, if Trollope had chosen to see a lady's face, nothing would have been easier.[9] His mother's friends and relatives would have had him in their houses. He might be a derelict young man with no obvious future, but Mrs Trollope was a figure – and, of course, some shrewd women would have perceived there was something in him. He could have had a reasonable social existence for the asking. He was too proud to ask. He wouldn't go among such people until he could go on his own terms and had made a name.[10]

Which leaves the mystery of his 'temptations'. One possibility, and a reasonable one, is that now and then he picked up prostitutes. London was not only a rough dirty town, great luxury mixed with great squalor, but its streets had a higher density of prostitutes than any capital in Europe. Much later in the century, the phenomenon deeply impressed Russian visitors, including Dostoevsky. Conspicuous luxury side by side with the grimmest squalor was no novelty to him, after Petersburg. The litter of the pavements was a mild shock, as it is to modern Russians. But wiping out all other sights, was something he had never seen before, in Russia, Germany, anywhere in Europe – the parade of prostitutes in the Haymarket, many of them young girls, thirteen or fourteen. Dostoevsky went home, prophesying apocalyptic doom for such a country.[11]

A young man on his own, unsure of himself, living with his own imagination, trapped, desperate? Why not the easiest release? It is one of the many things about him which we shall never know, but one would have to be untravelled to rule it out. Incidentally, in *The Vicar of Bullhampton*, written in his fifties, he gives a picture of a prostitute much more brotherly, candid and unhysterical than any other novelist of the period has managed to do.

There are other things which we shall never know with enough certainty for a court of law, but which oughtn't to puzzle us much. Mr James Pope Hennessy, usually sensible about biographical details, was worried because Trollope didn't tell us what as a young man in London he did with his evenings.[12] But in effect he does, expecting his readers to have an idea of how young men behave.

Prostitutes, Haymarket, c. 1860

There weren't many entertainments in the raw London of the 1830s. One can't drink away every night and, though alcohol was cheap, he and his friends couldn't have afforded it. Similarly with prostitutes. If that latter guess is right, it wouldn't have been a regular habit. No, the obvious answer is what he lets slip himself. He did a lot of reading. He improved his Latin and taught himself to read French. In English literature he was already familiar with the best English fiction, and so concentrated on poetry.[13]

While he read, in what must have been like a poor student's bedroom, his imagination couldn't help. The structured dreams, with their narrative and characters, weren't to be kept out of mind. He says that he never put pen to paper.[14] It is hard to believe him. It wouldn't be astonishing if he had tried to write verse, and discovered that it wasn't his *métier*. In any case, his first novel, still years in the future, turned out altogether more confident than is plausible for a sheer beginner: and so did his first pieces of journalism.

One other thing, for which there is no evidence whatever except what his own novels say with a plangency that moves us after more than a hundred years. There was a young woman who in his life played the part of Lily Dale in Eames's. She needn't have been at all like Lily Dale. She needn't have lived in squirearchical surroundings and been jilted by a social climber. She needn't have borne Trollope the kind of casual sisterly affection which Lily Dale bore Johnny Eames, or any affection at all. He may not have known her very well. But that there was a young woman whom he loved to distraction when he was miserable and obscure – and who probably didn't think much of him – doesn't admit of doubt. Trollope invented a great deal in his fiction, but there are some emotional states that no writer can invent.[15]

Some of those states cry out of passages when Eames is alone. They are not the best passages Trollope wrote, but they are some of the most naked, and anyone with an ear for confession knows that *the truth was like this, and not otherwise.*

At twenty-six he was rescued from his London desolation by a curious administrative accident. Post Office fieldwork was under the charge of officials called surveyors (a rank which continued to exist up to the Second World War), who lived in their region and presided over the mail service. There were twelve in all, and it was thought desirable to give them each a clerk, active enough to travel round the surveyor's locality. A vacancy had occurred for a surveyor's clerk in the west of Ireland. The pay, most of it made up of allowances, was good. At twenty-six Trollope's salary in London had slowly mounted to a hundred and forty pounds per annum. In Ireland he could reckon on four hundred, a sizeable salary in 1841. Strangely no one wanted the job.[16] Trollope went to his enemy the Secretary[17] and applied for it. According to Trollope the Secretary was so glad to be rid of him that he didn't object, and Trollope was appointed.

7

SEA-CHANGE

Trollope must be one of the few Englishmen whose lives have been changed for the better by going to Ireland. Dean Swift would have had something to say about that. The transmogrification in Trollope was spectacularly speedy. Within a year of crossing the Irish Sea he regarded himself as a fortunate and, in many ways, a happy man.[1] Already this was the best time of his life: not that that was overwhelming praise.

There were several objective reasons why he should feel his existence was transformed. He had a fair income to play with: that made a psychological, as well as a practical, difference. He was posted to Banagher on the Shannon, out on the Connaught border, and it was an agreeable little town. Of all the places in which Trollope lived, this is the one which would strike him as most familiar now: the long Irish main street, the pair of good houses, the affable ramshackle air.[2]

There was something ramshackle also about his superior, the Post Office surveyor for the west of Ireland. He was an amiable man who had a marked distaste for excessive exertion: Trollope, his new deputy, hadn't. That suited them both. It was only a matter of months before Trollope, as he said himself, had acquired the character of a thoroughly good public servant, which afterwards everyone assumed was his in perpetuity. The amiable surveyor ran a pack of hounds, but hadn't the energy to hunt himself. Trollope promptly bought a hunter and didn't desist from the sport until, very sadly, forty years later, he found himself too old. It became an obsessive passion of his, more so than most men feel for their favourite amusements. As he confesses, rather coyly, he couldn't resist dragging a hunting scene into almost any of his novels. Very spirited they are: but at times one feels a certain relief that Dostoevsky didn't develop a comparable passion for philately.

Hunting gave him another objective reason for content. It brought him easy-going fellowship of the kind, and with the range of people, which he had always longed for. He was at home with hard-riding convivial squires and farmers, most of them penurious. He hunted with the

Galway Blazers and the West Galway. The local gentry took him into their houses. William Gregory, who had pitied him at Harrow, now discovered a man who rode as dashingly as he did and entertained him at Coole.

Trollope liked both the Anglo-Irish and the Irish. He was one of the rare Englishmen who were actually fond of the real Irish. It helped that he always had a tenderness for the Catholic faith. If forced to choose between the Catholic communion and Presbyterianism, Trollope would have preferred the first. In this respect as in so many others, he was the

The Ward Hunt, by William Osborne. Trollope hunted with the Ward as well as with the Galway Blazers and West Galway

diametrical opposite of Dickens, who, living in Italy, had to control his disgust when forced to enter the door of a Catholic church.

Probably there was also a subjective reason for Trollope's liberation. Not even good luck changes a man's inner weather so totally overnight. He was just at the stage when he was ready and waiting for such a change. He was too robust a man, had too much strength and warmth of nature, to abide in passive despondency much longer. Depression, yes, he could struggle against that. Like many depressives, he had much capacity for enjoyment and it was ready to break out. It doesn't need

The Bank of Ireland and Convent (top) *and the Post Office,*
Banagher, c. *1900*

stressing that, a few months after he took up his job in Ireland, he met
his future wife and became secretly engaged.

To begin with, though, the first liberating agent was his work. He felt –
and this was a joy, as it wouldn't have been to a young man less humble –
that he was after all some use. By chance, he dropped into work he might
have been made for. It required common sense, some executive ability,
decisiveness, and much physical endurance. The amiable surveyor was
glad to perceive these qualities in his deputy. He relapsed into amiable
sloth, and let Trollope get on with it.

As has been mentioned before, the early Victorian Civil Service was
operating in a society still unorganized. In theory the surveyor, in practice his deputy Trollope, were executing tasks which haven't come anywhere near civil servants at their level this century. Trollope was riding
round, a big young man on a big horse (there were still no railways in
Ireland), investigating individual complaints – checking the accounts

of village postmasters – mapping the routes of postmen carrying letters – arranging for deliveries to lonely country houses. He loved it. He could see the results of his work, and was good at it. Incidentally, since he received extra allowances for each day spent away from his base, the more he travelled the larger his income. He loved that too.

But, though he loved those official visits – and went on doing so for many years – it has to be said that the same delight was not felt by all he visited. Village postmasters dreaded the sight of him. He had developed, or grown into, an official manner which was curiously unsympathetic and which became a characteristic of his career. In fact, it was the face that acquaintances met in his casual human relations. The manner was peremptory, aggressive, interrogatory, hectoring. It was the same with his superiors, for Trollope was the opposite of a time server, but not unnaturally it was more frightening, and more of an affront, to subordinates.

Some of the anecdotes are funny in a rough Victorian way: but nevertheless it was a strange defect in a man who was uniformly patient and delicately paternal with anyone for whom he cared. If the surveyor of Banagher hadn't been so inert, he might have told Trollope to show better manners. Conceivably, since this was the young man's first real job, it wouldn't have been too late.

However, the need for this façade – for it was that – cut very deep. It

Left *Village postman, 1856.* Right *Post boy, 1845*

was part of his attempt to hide his inner softnesses and to construct a world-confronting personality for himself. It deceived unperceptive people all his life. Bluff old Anthony. Tough old Anthony. Hearty old Anthony. He wouldn't have minded anyone thinking that.

Escott makes an interesting comment which doesn't appear elsewhere.[3] He wasn't in the least taken in by this bizarre manner and had a shrewd idea that it was a cover: but he also suggests that Trollope picked up this cover by copying the style of his own family and their friends, the High Anglican Wykehamists of the early nineteenth century. According to Escott, who knew similar people as old men, they were loud-voiced, given to barking, not a bit considerate in argument, assertive in ordinary human interchange. This strikes us today as distinctly unexpected, but Escott was nearer to them than we are. If he is right, Archdeacon Grantly in the flesh would, to begin with, have seemed less urbane than we have imagined.

As soon as Trollope was happy in his work – not totally happy, for he was reproaching himself that he had not begun to write, and time was getting on – he promptly got engaged. The girl, some years younger than he was, adds to all the things we don't know, should like to know, will never know, about Trollope's life. The hard facts we have could be written on the back of a postcard. Incidentally, she lived until 1917 and as a child the present writer could have met her. Which, apart from another example of literary continuity, is not specially consoling.

Trollope met his future wife at the seaside near Dublin in the summer of 1842. It didn't take them long to become engaged, but they couldn't get married for two years because, so Trollope says, they had no money except his income. The few hard facts about Rose Trollope are these. Her maiden name was Heseltine. Her father was the manager of a bank in Rotherham, Yorkshire, but only of a local branch. Mrs Trollope almost certainly viewed the marriage with cheerful snobbish disapproval. Rose was by Trollope standard lower middle class, brought no money with her, and presumably began her married life with traces of a Yorkshire accent. Mrs Trollope referred to her as Anthony's excellent little wife.[4]

The affairs of Rose's father culminated some years after the marriage in a good Victorian financial melodrama. He was a respected Rotherham citizen until it was suddenly realized that he had made away with several thousand pounds. He had to skip to France – to Le Havre, rather a strange resort to exile oneself to – and died there in his fifties.

Rose was very small, something like five feet high. Observers thought her distinctly pretty. She went prematurely white. She bore a son two years after marrying, another eighteen months later, and then no more. As soon as the Trollopes became prosperous, she was noticed for being beautifully dressed. She was efficient, transcribed her husband's hand-

*Kingstown, fashionable resort near Dublin – meeting place of
Trollope and Rose*

writing, and handled his literary affairs when he was abroad. Late in
life he told his son Henry that he trusted her judgment totally in all
literary matters, and advised Henry to do the same.[5]

She was the only person other than Trollope's publishers to see a
Trollope novel (or part of one) before publication. There are about a
dozen letters of hers in existence, staccato, competent, bright-witted.

That is about all we know of her for certain. The rest has to be guessed.
It is remarkable enough how little Trollope himself occurs in Victorian
memoirs, much less than his brother Tom. Yet in his years of great success, the Trollopes were prize guests in great houses. They liked going,
but Rose, though perfectly easy in society, seems to have moved about

as though she were invisible. When there were comments, they were on nothing but her clothes.

Among the Trollope relatives a generation later, there were vestigial hints that she was not specially liked. Trollope, some years after the marriage, said that she had made him so continually happy that he wondered at it, and scarcely dared hope that the luck would last. We are left with speculations. The present writer has to intrude his own: which is that she was very far from negligible, sharp-tongued, witty, a more coherent and in many ways tougher personality than her husband. Possibly too much so to give him a marriage ideal for his temperament. With women he had a strong paternal-cum-amorous streak. He liked to teach, fire instructions, scold, and this – it is a fair bet – was part of his erotic nature.

It is difficult to imagine that kind of love-play with Rose Trollope. It was a good marriage, no wife could have been more loyal, but the feeling remains – it may be altogether false – that he was not entirely liberated. His letters and references to Kate Field do suggest by contrast that there his nerves at last were absolutely free.

On the other hand, he owes Rose a greater debt than an utterly stable marriage, the services of a first-rate private critic, and a lifetime support. People don't seem to have wondered how the marvellous young women in his novels were born. A whole string of them, from Lucy Robarts, Mary Thorne, down to Lady Mabel Grex, are witty, high spirited, strong willed, so much cleverer than their men. Startlingly for their period, they are quite unashamed and free and easy about their senses and desires.

Think of Lucy Robarts – the best of his well-behaved girls – ruminating about her love for Lord Lufton. She says in effect that he is a decent young man, honourable, kind, not too bright: but what she can't resist about him are the charms of his looks and his fine straight legs.[6] Lady Mabel Grex is worth ten of Lord Silverbridge and Frank Tregear and knows it: but she also knows (though she is a very young woman) that she is at the mercy of her passion for Tregear. Does anyone believe that when they were twenty their relation was innocent? It is doubtful whether Trollope did.

Trollope was an intuitive man with a great deal of psychological imagination. He could make do, in a creative sense, with very little. Given a hint or a start, and he could develop a realistic character. But, of course, he did need a hint or a start. No novelist – no good novelist, that is – can produce his people out of a complete vacuum. One asks again: where did that gallery of women begin? They are so different from the women of any English writer of his time. Yet when he was writing the novels in which they first stand out in all their cleverness and will – and their cheek – he can't have had many opportunities for intimate observation. It is obvious that they are most intimately observed, far more devotedly so than the young men.

There seem to be only two likely sources. The son of Mrs Trollope – even a neglected son, perhaps more so on that account – couldn't avoid realizing that a woman might possess will and energy as much as any man. And a certain kind of optimistic hardness which is sometimes a feature of Trollopian women. Nevertheless Mrs Trollope, to judge from her books, wasn't witty nor psychologically acute. She had a sort of period sarcasm, but none of the peculiar tantalizing appeal, at the same time subtle, funny and derisive, of the best Trollope girls.

There is a second source conceivable. Trollope had excellent opportunities for observing one. It is a somewhat obvious suggestion, but that young woman was his wife.[7]

Rose Trollope

8

BUILDING A CHARACTER

Soon after he had become engaged Trollope started to write his first novel. His own account of the experience is one of the features of the autobiography where we have to suspend a good deal of disbelief. The contrasts between light and dark are altogether too sharp, the acceptance of failure before the radiant success to come. He couldn't resist colouring a good story. No writer, however much he trusted Trollope's probity, which was in essential matters absolute, could accept that all this happened, subjective feelings included, as in old age Trollope liked to imagine that it happened.

He tells us once again, using the same phrase, that before September 1843 he had never 'put pen to paper'. Once again one wonders.[1] There follows a passage which can be trusted. He retained, he says, the 'still cherished determination to become a writer of novels...'

> I do not think I much doubted my own intellectual sufficiency for the writing of a readable novel. What I did doubt was my own industry and the chances of a market. The vigour necessary to prosecute two professions at the same time is not given to everyone, and it was only lately that I had found the vigour necessary for one. But still the purpose was strong within me.[2]

So he began. Like all realistic novelists – like Tolstoi, Dostoevsky, Proust, Galdós – Trollope needed the reassurance of something he knew at first-hand to set his imagination going. Just as in his daydreams he had always started from a base of everday fact. The Leinster countryside – not in itself exciting – had stimulated him, and the prospect of a derelict country house. Thus he got going on *The Macdermots of Ballycloran*. He didn't get going as fluently or as obsessively as in his later years, rather less so than comparable writers with their first novels. He was only halfway through when, in twelve months' time, he married.

The second half went a little faster. His wife knew all about it, and began her lifetime's job of literary confidante and critic. In his deepest concerns, he was like other men with highly developed sensibility to anyone round them, secretive, often morbidly so, as is obvious from his autobiography. But he couldn't have concealed from her what this novel meant to him, what he hoped for, and what he thought of it.

It is an exceptionally good novel. Owing to the crass misjudgment of Michael Sadleir,[3] it has continued to be under-rated in England, and it has taken the fresh eyes of young American critics to see just how good it is. It is clumsily constructed, though the narrative line is better than in most Trollope novels. It shows, already highly developed, many of his major psychological gifts, of which more later. It also shows, what is suppressed or understated in nearly all the famous books, his dark sense of life. It ought to rank, not with the five or six master works, but not too far below.

He must have known some of this, at least part of the time. He was a realistic man and not a confident one. But also he was a writer at the beginning of his career, and human – and, though he would have a writer's qualms and in his case more than normal self-doubt, these would be flooded out by euphoria and magnificent expectations.

There is absolutely no such memory in the autobiography. Instead he tells us one of his most pathetically funny anecdotes. The Trollopes were now installed, for the first time with some appearance of prosperity, in a large apartment in Clonmel,[4] a new district, a different surveyor. That was a change for the better. The town was bigger and livelier, the company more sophisticated, Trollope's Post Office reputation more than secure.

Book finished, manuscript carefully guarded, they went to enjoy a family holiday with his sister Cecilia and her husband John Tilley. This was in July 1845. Four years later Cecilia was to die of the family disease. For the moment she was well and happy. Her husband was an up-and-coming civil servant who finished as Secretary of the Post Office. He had been a contemporary of Trollope's[5] in the office at St Martin's-le-Grand, and they were lifelong friends. They were living in a house in Cumberland, taken over from Mrs Trollope, one of her discarded staging posts on the way to Florence.

Mrs Trollope and Tom had come over from Florence (where they were not yet installed but were surveying the ground) to spend the summer at their former house, and those two and the Tilleys were all assembled to greet Trollope and Rose. For once Trollope may have felt warm and welcome inside his family. If so, as soon as he announced (one guesses, with defensive bluffness) that he had written a novel, he didn't feel so for long.

Their response appears to have been sheer stupefaction. Mrs Trollope, brisk and active as ever, said she would show it to a publisher – but that it would be better if she didn't read it herself. Trollope remarks:

I knew that she did not give me credit for the sort of cleverness necessary for such work. I could see in the faces and hear in the voices of my friends who were around me in the house in Cumberland – my mother, my sister, my brother-in-law, and, I think, my brother, that they had not expected me to come out as one of the family authors. There were three or four in the field before me, and it seemed almost absurd that another should wish to add himself to the number. My mother had become one of the most popular authors. My brother had commenced, and had become fairly well paid for his work.[6] My sister had also written a novel which was at the time in manuscript...[7]

It would be good to know Rose Trollope's opinion of that curious scene. Perhaps Trollope was being hypersensitive – any writer would have had his nerve ends exposed. Mrs Trollope's mixture of businesslike efficiency and total lack of sensibility does take an elevated place in the history of literary obtuseness. (Compare Belinsky, pathologically tired but reading *Poor Folk* with fierce intensity.[8])

She was as good as her promise, though, and two years later the book was published. Here Trollope's statements have to be read with affectionate suspicion. He writes:

> I can with truth declare that I expected nothing and I got nothing. Nor did I expect fame, or even acknowledgement. I was sure that the book would fail, and it did fail most absolutely. I never heard of a person reading it in those days. If there was any notice taken of it by any critic of the day, I did not see it ... I do not remember that I felt in any way disappointed or hurt. I am quite sure that no word of complaint passed my lips. I think I may say that after the publication I never said a word about the book, even to my wife.[9]

Unless Trollope was different in kind from any writer who has ever lived, or as far as that goes from any young man who has made any kind of effort whatever, almost none of that can conceivably be true: and where it can be checked some of it appears to be factually untrue. Commercially, there isn't any question, the book did nothing. There is no surprise in that. First novels were as difficult to sell in the 1840s as they are today. A reasonable analogy would be some late twentieth-century Trollope producing, as his first novel, a tragic story about Northern Ireland. It wouldn't stand much of a chance. He would be lucky to get it published at all.

On the other hand, the press was distinctly good, more serious and perhaps more perceptive than it would be likely to be today. There were nothing like so many places where novels were reviewed, but *The Macdermots* was praised in influential papers such as the *Spectator* and the *Athenaeum*.[10] It would have been extraordinary if none of this reception had been conveyed to Trollope. It was warm enough to encourage most

Above *Cork*, where Trollope's sons later went to one of their first schools. Right *Bianconi* long car. These linked all the market towns in the south and west of Ireland. Trollope met Carlo Bianconi in Clonmel in 1845 and was influenced by his successful transport system in re-organizing the Irish postal services

writers. If we believe him, what were his friends doing, friends such as John Merivale, with whom he had actually explored the house which was the starting point of the novel? They would have been abnormally cold fish not to drop a line: and there is plenty of evidence that Merivale was a good, affectionate and literate friend.

Trollope admits no whisper of news from London. He continues:

> The fact that I had written and published it [*The Macdermots*], and that I was writing another, did not in the least interfere with my life or with my determination to make the best I could of the Post Office. In Ireland I think that no one knew I had written a novel. But I went on writing.[11]

That was authentic. In those simple sentences Trollope is saying something important about himself, not falsified by romantic darkening. As to the facts, he did publish the second novel, *The Kellys and The O'Kellys*, the year after the first. It also lost money for the publisher and had some amiable reviews. Trollope, who knew his major gift with complete accuracy, didn't know – and never did know until he died – what he couldn't begin to do. He cast round for other literary forms: an historical novel (extremely bad), a guide book to Ireland (probably good, but not published), an historical play (unspeakably bad). He couldn't realize that a subject he hadn't seen with his own acute eyes wasn't available to him.

Meanwhile, as he firmly says, he was doing his duty by the Post Office, and, like the good official he had become, doing more than his duty. He would probably have disliked losing his reputation there more bitterly than the failure of a novel. This may seem strange to those conditioned by purely aesthetic values. Trollope was a true artist, but, as with Chekhov, he would have been contemptuous of making that an excuse for ignoring other abjections. Art as the prime and only value, or as the justification for a mish-mash of living, to those two wouldn't have formed a code open to decent men.

Further, Trollope was living within an institution where he was now respected. He had suffered so long from receiving no respect. He was one of those who imbibe confidence from institutions and feel excessively deprived if that confidence isn't returned. Lack of promotion at the Post Office (he didn't become a full surveyor till rather late) wounded him when he was already conceiving the Barchester novels: and when he was one of the best-known novelists in England he was – see later, chapter 15 – much more enraged at not getting the Assistant Secretaryship (the number two job) than he was at any literary reverse.

That was, of course, years in the future. But it is foreshadowed in that statement of his about the beginning of his double working life. He is saying, in fact, that at that age, thirty-two, he had stabilized his character or perhaps at last had managed to build one. He had disliked himself a good deal, too much for any kind of self-respect. Now he had by effort made something a bit more respect-worthy.

He could look at himself in a psychological mirror without revulsion – perhaps he still didn't like looking at himself in an optical mirror. The character he had built he could now live with: and to him far more than to most men that was a cardinal step in his entire existence.

By character here is meant something different from inherent nature. Inherent nature – Trollope's insight was clear and bleak, as about anything in the human condition – wasn't capable of being changed. It didn't change in him. Towards the end of his life, as will be seen – after an eventful career, full of what others regarded as success and fame, which he himself felt sometimes had been a bit of a triumph – he let out a cry of misgiving as distressed as any in the past.

No, nature wasn't to be changed. But character, by will and effort and luck, might be: character being the behaviour which one manages to keep to, the front or persona which one shows to the world and, just as important, to oneself. To an extent, personality, which is a fusion of nature and character, can be changed too, although perceptive people will see below the character to what lies underneath.

The character which Trollope wished to construct for himself was much simpler than what he really was, or, to use the wretched modern jargon, what he was in his authenticity. He wanted to be an honourable man, relied on by his fellows, as kind and given to generous actions as he could aspire to. He was brave by nature, morally and physically, and hoped his character might be braver. He wanted to be honest, straightforward and live by a gentleman's code.

All this appears to an age which has abandoned moral striving to be both priggish and dull. If he became dull as he built his character, that was a price he would certainly have been prepared to pay. It is usually true that a man who tries to discipline his character, and suppress the malice and ill-nature, is likely to seem stuffier, less spontaneous, less good company. It is the person who does not control a spiteful tongue who is (on the instant, until he goes away and practises on oneself) the best fun. This is one of the minor manifestations of original sin.

Gruff, abrupt, not always (except with women) socially pacifying, Trollope was showing the strain of building a character. But in his early thirties it was a character he could accept, and it didn't alter much. A satisfactory marriage – perhaps more than satisfactory – had helped consolidate it. Part of the persona, if the guess about his diffidence is right, would be that of the substantial married man in the midst of his family.

It was one of the signs of his character, so arduously struggled for, that

[69]

he made, and kept on making, rigid codes for himself which he rigidly kept to. A typical one occurred when his second novel disappeared into oblivion.

> [And] I made up my mind then that should I continue this trade of authorship I would neither ask for nor deplore criticism nor would I ever thank a critic for praise, or quarrel with him, even in my own heart, for censure. To this rule I have adhered with absolute strictness, and this rule I would recommend to all young authors. What can be got by touting among the critics is never worth the ignominy. The same may of course be said of all things acquired by ignominious means. But in this matter it is so easy to fall into the dirt.[12]

Don't think that he didn't know the temptations. He knew all the temptations. Coexisting with this implacable persona was a nature of quite abnormal subtlety. Otherwise, of course, he couldn't have written his books, and penetrated so many characters, shared in their frailties and evils. Very few writers, and probably very few men, have ever lived with such complicated undercurrents of intuition and empathy, which is why he, in his own behaviour, controlled them so harshly.

In his own time a few perceptive persons realized this.[13] They met the noisy blustering man, boomingly straightforward, patriarchal, the personification of Victorian masculine honour, and they noticed that beneath that façade dwelt a mass of what they thought of as quivering 'feminine' sensitivity. That was the observation of Escott, his first biographer, who spent a good deal of time with Trollope when he was old.[14]

The diagnosis has been repeated since. It isn't a bad shot, but can be misleading. First, we ought to forget the sexual adjective. This special combination of labile nature, of both intuition and insight, of the ability to enter imaginatively into others' lives is very rare in both men and women, and possibly as rare in one sex as the other (though, if women possess it, they sometimes have had more chance to develop it). And then, that kind of shorthand doesn't seem to touch the essential point of such a nature.

Trollope seriously lacked ego. He had nothing of the billiard-ball-like inner certainty which takes many men, and some great writers (Goethe, Dickens), crashingly through their lives. His necessity to build a character, his devices to escape melancholy through unremitting activity, were attempts to reinforce his ego. Often he was working to push away the dark. He insisted on saying that his had, since his youth, been an unusually happy life. That was shouting against the dark. It would have been more correct to say that it had been an unusually eventful and interesting one.

There were major compensations on the other side. People whose egos are as fragile as his are often unusually tender and sympathetic. Two pleasant examples would be Sydney Smith[15] and Chekhov. Certain kinds of intuition are open to them as not to others. Trollope's specific psychological delicacy depended fundamentally on this lack of ego. He couldn't have understood his great characters, Mr Crawley, Palliser, perhaps not even his splendid girls, if his ego had been harder. No writer, and no man, can have all the psychological equipment he could wish for. If one is as adamantine as Dante, one can't be as empathetic as Shakespeare.

If you want to tell the deepest and most exploratory truths about other people, you may have to accept a weakness in ego: which in turn may mean that your own life will be more fractured, and your own personality less effective. Less effective – not less strong or impressive, but not so defined or all of a piece.

All the evidence suggests that this was true of Trollope even when, in his thirties, his character was formed, and it remained true until he died. There is a significant pointer all through what he writes of himself. He had made himself resolute: but he never lets himself admit what he was hoping. In his thirties success was not far away. Not long after the period just discussed, even a realistic and apprehensive man might have gambled upon it. He must have had brilliant hopes. He gives no sign that he ever did. Yet a writer, particularly a writer who had had to wait so long, couldn't go on without hope. It looks as though he was being superstitious, and, quite unlike his mother in her cheerful struggles, touching wood.

9
ARRIVAL

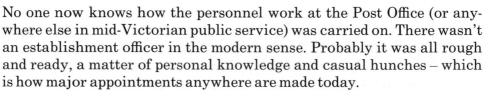

No one now knows how the personnel work at the Post Office (or anywhere else in mid-Victorian public service) was carried on. There wasn't an establishment officer in the modern sense. Probably it was all rough and ready, a matter of personal knowledge and casual hunches – which is how major appointments anywhere are made today.

Anyway, though the Post Office didn't treat Trollope handsomely, they had a shrewd idea of his abilities, and found ingenious ways of using them. In 1851, when he was thirty-six, no literary success except a little invisible esteem, they invented a new job for him – or discovered that there was a job which no one else was doing.

Rural letter deliveries – had no one looked at them? It was crazily unsystematic and hit-and-miss. A farmhouse six miles west of Exeter could receive its letters every two days: one the same distance to the east would wait a week. The letter carriers (i.e. postmen) were none too industrious, and anyway there was no one to plan their routes. Deputy Surveyor Trollope – in the Post Office records he is called by his unexalted rank, Surveyor's Clerk Trollope – was the man to put this right. For two years he was seconded to the south-west of England, charged with getting rural deliveries in order. Which he did.

Once more he loved the job. It was hard on his wife, as they moved from town to town. It got in the way of the boys' schooling. But for him it meant immersing himself in a practical exercise where again he could see the results. It also meant meeting all kinds of people, parsons, farmers, squires, labourers, a cross-section of the population of what was still an agricultural slice of England.

Opposite *Salisbury Cathedral, by John Constable, 1823. 'Whilst wandering . . . round the purlieus of the cathedral I conceived the story of* The Warden.' *Autobiography. Overleaf Sunday Morning, The Walk from the Church, by Richard Redgrave, 1846. Think of Plumstead Episcopi, maybe after a firm sermon from the Archdeacon*

He did it all on horseback, riding forty miles a day. He was riding forty miles a day, in order to save postmen walking more than sixteen miles a day: which involved exploring field paths, cart tracks all the way from Cornwall to Monmouthshire. During this tour of duty he suggested that letter boxes, the ancestors of pillar boxes, should be experimented with in Jersey – 'Mr Trollope's suggestion', as the Post Office officially called it, and a nice one to be remembered by. He was proud of it.[1]

This activity in south-west England was the kind of open-air physical life which suited him. He could forget about writing for the time being. It may have been the latent period that he needed. This region of England is still one of the prettiest in the country, and in the 1850s it must have been a visual delight. The Georgian houses (by which Trollope wasn't moved) were sedately established by now. Victorian Gothic hadn't yet spread much in the countryside. The farms were trim and prosperous, it was twenty years in the future before the great agricultural depression ravaged them.

Trollope was far too detached an observer not to take account of the defacing spots. The cottages of agricultural labourers were often singularly unlike the idyllic pictures. They were more likely to be lean-tos or hovels. And the agricultural labourers themselves must have depressed him. It was part of his region (Wiltshire, Gloucestershire, Monmouth) where Anglophile Americans like F.L. Olmsted were shocked by what they found.[2] For ignorance, dullness, lack of vitality, stupid apathy, the Americans reported that they had seen nothing so bad anywhere in Europe. Trollope himself, in his travels through Connemara and Leinster, had commented that the peasants of pre-famine Ireland were very much brighter and cleverer than their English counterparts.[3]

Still, this pretty bit of England had a look of permanence, and the labourers and their hovels hadn't. The great cathedrals (Salisbury, Worcester, Exeter, Wells, Winchester) stood as they had since the Middle Ages. The cathedral closes, more than the stately Christian edifices, may have brought to Trollope both excitement and repose, the kind of feeling a writer experiences when, before he realizes it, something is setting his creative imagination free. He tells us that one summer evening, walking round the 'purlieus' of Salisbury Cathedral, he was struck by the story of *The Warden*.

Opposite *Gentleman in a Railway Carriage, by James Tissot, mid-1870s. At first in the south-west Trollope travelled everywhere on horseback; later: 'I found that I passed in railway-carriages very many hours of my existence . . . I made for myself therefore a little tablet, and found that I could write as quickly in a railway-carriage as I could at my desk.'* Autobiography

[73]

Village postman, 1867. Inset *On Trollope's initiative, the first letter boxes in the British Isles were erected in the Channel Islands. This one, dating from c. 1854, is in Union Street, St Peter Port, Guernsey*

Those purlieus were the close and the opulent clerical houses. One knows that he was struck by something deeper and richer than the plot, story, or argument of that novel. It may have happened by chance: but creative chances are no good except to someone ready and waiting for them. He really knew his gift, it was evident in his first book: but now he had been given the most important present a writer can receive, the realization of how to make it work.

[74]

Most of *The Warden* was, as it happened, written in Belfast. That was an advantage. He was one of those novelists, and that includes nearly all the best, who write more deeply about their chosen scene when they get a good long way removed from it. But he didn't like being transferred to Ulster. He was also irked at not being able to finish cleanly his English assignment. With the gusto of a genuine public servant, he says: 'I should have liked to ride over the whole country and to have sent a rural-post letter carrier to every parish, every village, every hamlet, and every grange in England.'[4]

In 1854, at the age of thirty-nine, he was at last promoted full Surveyor. This he reported proudly to his mother, which makes nonsense of previous protestations that, though aggrieved, he hadn't worried much at being so often and pointedly passed over.[5] Now he asked his mother to rejoice with him.[6] It is significant that, in all his letters to her, he never once referred to his literary plans and prospects. He did want her to recognize that he was doing pretty well in his official career. Which, as has been mentioned before, gave him more pangs, more flickers of exaltation, than the switchback ride of his writing. Until he was old, and letting his reserve slip, he didn't write anything so excited about a piece of literary good fortune as in this letter about his promotion.

There were practical benefits. The salary was seven hundred a year, and allowances seem to have brought this up to about eight hundred, which was a good professional income in the 1850s and much later. (Senior professors at major universities got no more until after the First World War.) Further, he could begin to make his own terms about his district. He extricated himself from Belfast, and for the first time in their married life the Trollopes had, just outside Dublin, a largish house to themselves – though, it is true, a singularly ugly one. There he had reasons for happiness, and there he wrote some good books – and one atrociously bad one, fortunately not published.

The Warden appeared, after delays unusual in Victorian publishing, in 1855. It didn't sell much. Sales of novels, even novels now among the most famous in the language, were very small in the mid-nineteenth century. The reading public, except for magazines, was minuscule. That allowed for, *The Warden* seems to have been more talked about than bought. A thousand copies were printed, and in four years seven hundred were sold. Nevertheless Trollope says that he 'soon felt that it had not failed as the others had failed'.[7]

It was well and seriously reviewed. Critics quarrelled with Trollope's moral ambiguity or neutrality, which later was thought of as one of his greatest strengths. Stern Victorian liberals said seriously that he wasn't hard enough on time-worn abuses. He had used a topical story which had been something of a sensation (as with the starting points of other famous novels),[8] and the liberal critics knew about this particular abuse. Yet they noticed, sometimes not being sure what they were noticing, how he could understand, represent, see into his major characters. That should have been equally evident in the Irish novels, but Archdeacon Grantly was the first Trollopian personage to make his three-dimensional presence felt.

Some of Trollope's virtues were clear. His psychological mastery, his moral balance, they couldn't be altogether escaped. His frailties were clear too, and the critics were on stronger ground when they picked them out. When he wasn't trying, he was both witty and humorous, so subtly that people who have to hear a writer announce that a joke is coming have obtusely missed his sophisticated fun.

That humour can be seen in *The Warden*, though not with the constant ripple that runs through some of his finest novels. That was when he wasn't trying. When he really was trying, he could be dreadfully facetious. He never seems to have known how unfunny he could be. His attempts at jocular attacks on Carlyle (Doctor Pessimist Anti-cant) and Dickens (Mr Popular Sentiment) make one squirm to this day. As also does his life-long habit of giving facetious surnames to minor characters – Dr Fillgrave, Sir Omicron Pie – whom he then often portrays with complete psychological realism. This trick of nomenclature seems to have given simple delight to other nineteenth-century novelists. Dickens did a lot, presumably decided it wasn't that entrancing, controlled himself and then again succumbed. Dostoevsky sometimes did it. But Trollope, the most scrupulously realistic of them all, was the worst offender.

After the reception of *The Warden*, Trollope had the feeling, the pricking at the fingers' ends, that writers know, if they're lucky enough. Come hell, come high water, he was going to be read. That didn't prevent him wasting time on one of his most fatuous misjudgments. He thought he would emulate Carlyle and make a stir. The minor facts that he had no use whatever for Carlyle and no talent whatever for polemic, didn't deter him. His publisher's reader was incredulous: was this dismal essay by the author of *The Warden*? Longmans firmly turned it down, and, sobriety returning, Trollope, at peace in his Donnybrook house, began to write *Barchester Towers*.

Opposite above *The White Hart, Sherfield-on-Loddon, near Basingstoke. Photography by W. Savage, 1856. 'I did my business after a fashion in which no other official man has worked, at least for many years. I went almost everywhere on horseback.'* Autobiography. Opposite centre *Agricultural labourer's cottage, c. 1850s.* Opposite below *Masters and Brothers at Hall, St Cross, Winchester. It is rather strange to imagine Warden Harding's charges in top hats. Photograph by W. Savage, 1860s*

Original cover of The Warden

It took him a year and a half, even though he was perfecting his remarkable practice of writing in railway trains. Though it is a long book, he wouldn't have required such a time later in his career. He enjoyed writing it, and he pretty certainly had the subliminal feeling that his enjoyment was going to be shared. He seems to have been confident all the time he was writing, confident that the book was all right, and that he was nearly there. He remained confident as it came out. With complete justification.

The actual sales of the book, though larger than those of *The Warden*, were not spectacular. The press was not spectacular either. Still, Trollope says quietly, 'it was one of the novels which novel readers were called upon to read.'[9] In fact word was going round that here was a new and important talent. He had arrived. He had had to wait a long time.

Over twenty years, he informs us, *The Warden* and *Barchester Towers* together brought him seven hundred and twenty-seven pounds, eleven shillings and threepence.[10] Not very much. But, after *Barchester Towers*, sizeable money for the next Barchester novel was only a couple of years away. From 1857 onwards, which was the year of publication of *Barchester Towers*, Trollope was a successful professional writer.[11]

That was the year of publication of *Little Dorrit* and also the year of Matthew Arnold's famous inaugural lecture at Oxford. Not long afterwards, Arnold, with all his considerable weight of physique and mentality, was regretting how low was the present state of English creative writing.[12] Such a generalization is easier to make when one isn't inhibited by reading the creative writing in question. When Arnold published it (in 1865), he could have read, say, *Little Dorrit, Adam Bede, Great Expectations, The Last Chronicle of Barset*. Who believes that he had done so?[13]

The Close Gate, Salisbury, by C. S. Sargent c. 1852

10
AT THE BISHOP'S BEDSIDE

Barchester Towers has gone further and wider than any other of Trollope's novels, attracted more readers and been more continually popular. This has led some of his most serious modern admirers to under-value it – just as modern Dickensians, seeing *Little Dorrit, Bleak House, Our Mutual Friend* as the great books, under-rate *The Pickwick Papers* or *Martin Chuzzlewit*. Looked at with fresh eyes, *Barchester Towers* is a very good book. Some things, in delicacy, depth and power, Trollope did better later, but at the bleakest estimate it would rank among his best half dozen novels.

Barchester Towers has one of the most penetrating first chapters in all fiction, so quietly done, so truthful in tone, that attention has flickered over it. The old bishop is dying. The doctors say he may die any hour now. His son, Archdeacon Grantly, is at his bedside. Grantly loves his father, who has done him nothing but good.

In London the government is about to fall. If the bishop dies before it happens they will appoint a successor who will vote Tory in the Lords. (That is absolutely realistic: Melbourne appointed only Whig bishops, Peel only Tories, John Russell only Whigs, and so on. This party be-haviour was taken for granted until much later in the century.) That is, it is effectively certain that Archdeacon Grantly will be given his father's place. If however the bishop survives and the Whigs come in, they will appoint one of their own.

Grantly is an affectionate but ambitious man. At the bedside, he knows that he is wishing for his father to die. He begs to be forgiven, he tries to suppress what he is desiring, he summons up a prayer. The scene dis-solves into beautifully modulated, ironic comedy. It turns out that the government had already fallen that morning. The bishop dies the same day but Grantly cannot get the job.

None of his contemporaries is on record as noticing how ruthless, under the unstressed surface, that opening really is. Remember Arch-deacon Grantly is a decent man, a child of this world but also firm in his religion. Trollope has left us in no doubt in *The Warden*, and increasingly in this novel and through the Barchester series, that Grantly is one of the author's favourite characters. At moments the author may have felt a touch of resemblance between himself and Grantly. Trollope is saying, without fuss, this is what so many of us are like, this is part of being human. *Hypocrite lecteur*, don't flatter yourself. He says this very often, in many forms, but he is not hectoring us, only telling us to look out for the truth.

Nothing in the rest of *Barchester Towers* is as sharp-edged as that, but it is continuously stirring with psychological attention. There isn't anything of a plot in the narrow sense, as there is in *The Warden*. After his first novels, Trollope didn't take much trouble about plots. He says that he couldn't think of them, but that is more of his false modesty. He knew that the kind of novels he was fitted for were much more satisfactory without streamlined plots.

He was a master of narrative, propelling us from page to page by a flood of detailed invention, using as a rule simple and day-by-day materials. This was a legacy of all that practice with his realistic daydreams.

In *Barchester Towers (a)* the inner narrative is sustained by the marital future of Eleanor Bold, daughter of the old Warden, widow of the

Rev. J. W. Peers, Vicar of Tetsworth, Oxon, and family, by John Bridges, 1854. This may suggest some of Trollope's more prosperous clergy, such as Archdeacon Grantly when younger

[81]

idealistic protester in the previous novel, (*b*) the outer narrative is sustained by a power struggle between two cathedral parties, the new bishop and his wife Mrs Proudie, the chaplain Slope and fellow evangelicals on one side, the archdeacon and his High Anglican friends on the other.

In the comedy of (*b*), where Trollope isn't using his deepest insight, he doesn't pretend to be impartial. He doesn't like the Evangelicals any more than Grantly does, and yet some observer-artist over his shoulder makes him, almost against his will, suggest that Slope, the person he loathes most, is actually a formidable man.

There are some other ambiguities in *Barchester Towers* which run through his later Barsetshire novels. He doesn't spend any time on theological arguments: yet at the period of the novel Anglican clergymen in general and the educated public at large couldn't keep off them. Trollope's excuse for ignoring them, that he didn't have any acquaintance with clergymen, can be dismissed. Of course he did: and any man as well read and inquisitive as he was couldn't have missed the controversy. It was rather like someone in politics a century later not mentioning that there was a mild tension between communism and anti-

The Rector's Garden, Queen of the Lilies, by Atkinson Grimshaw, 1877. Not grand enough for Framley Parsonage, *but the girl would fit*

communism. Trollope must have known, as well as any man in England, that there was a profound conflict as to whether textual criticism of the Bible was to be permitted for Christians. He must also have known that some of the clergymen he most admires in his books (Arabin, Crawley, as well as non-intellectuals such as Robarts and Grantly) would inevitably have had to come down on the losing and suppressive side.

He hints at none of this. In fact, neither in his books nor his personal statements does he hint at what he himself believed. In later life he occasionally went to church, but his only overt step was, when he was helping start *The Fortnightly Review*, to insist on excluding articles which might deny the divinity of Christ.[1] One mustn't read the twentieth century back into him. But he was both sceptical and secretive and it seems not unlikely that, alone with himself, he came to believe rather little.

On the other hand, in formal terms, including ritual and social acquaintanceships, his sympathies were all with the high-church party. There is no doubt about that, and there is equally no doubt that this cut right across his political sympathies. In all the Barsetshire novels he is, as Victorian politicians would have called it, crossing his vote. In politics he was a Whiggish liberal, conservative about social matters, genuinely liberal about racial issues and (unlike most English intellectuals) the American Civil War. Eleven years after *Barchester Towers* he stood as a Liberal candidate for Parliament.

National politics and Church of England politics were still not separated from each other. Liberals were anti-tractarian, low church, trying to keep in touch with contemporary rational thought. (Bishop Proudie, if one forgets his wife and Slope, was a perfectly reasonable Liberal appointment.) Tories were high church, soft on Rome, devoted to extremes of doctrine about, say, absolute regeneration in baptism. Bishops' votes in the Upper House were important, and neither side considered losing such a vote to be sensible politics. All the clergymen Trollope writes of with real affection must have been Tories in politics, and, judged by their churchmanship, often extreme Tories, relics of eighteenth-century Jacobitism. He was on the wrong side – or, more exactly, as so often he was, balancing between the conflicting forces of his time.

There is just one factual impossibility in *Barchester Towers*, as ecclesiastical historians have pointed out.[2] Usually he took care, as he did later about Westminster politics. The sole impossibility is the offer of the Deanery of Barchester to Francis Arabin. Deaneries were Crown appointments, that is, were made by the Prime Minister. They weren't as important as bishoprics, but were much competed for, nice bits of patronage for the party in power.[3] In the novel, the party in power was

Croquet Party at Rev. H. Lee's. Photo by W. Savage, 1860s.
Compare the croquet party at The Small House at Allington

that which had appointed Bishop Proudie. It was quite impossible that the same party should appoint a high churchman (actually a churchman as high as they came, a tractarian) and a political enemy. Did Trollope forget? No one knew this kind of official jobbing more accurately. Of course, for artistic reasons it was highly desirable that Arabin should be installed as dean.

There is no indication in anything Trollope wrote, either at the time or in retrospect, that he felt exhilaration or any other of the triumphant emotions when success came at last. One might expect it to have been sweet. This was what he had craved for in his youthful misery. It had come late, much later than to any other major Victorian novelist. Dickens had been famous at twenty-four, Thackeray, George Eliot, Charlotte Brontë, by their mid-thirties. Wilkie Collins was just about to follow them in spectacular fashion. At the publication of *Barchester Towers* Trollope was forty-two. Maybe that was too old to get the full taste of what was happening, or maybe he was still too superstitious to admit that after all things were going right.

It is possible that he celebrated in a cryptic manner which we can interpret for ourselves. For he did something creatively perverse, and, perhaps, a little moving. Barset was open to him. He had a whole cast of characters already created. He had only to go on with the Barsetshire novels. But he didn't, at least not immediately. He turned back to his youth.

He turned back, but transformed it and transformed himself. *The Three Clerks* was his next book, and some of the setting was Trollope's own first years at the Post Office. A good many of Charlie Tudor's goings on, the farcical entrance examination, the imbroglios with barmaids, the gin-soaked evenings, happened – we know or can guess – to Trollope himself. Nevertheless Charlie Tudor isn't Trollope in the sense that John Eames is. He is much happier and much luckier. He gets into troubles and miseries, but emerges triumphant. A nice girl, of impeccable lady-like origins, loves him. He makes a start at writing and is praised by everyone round him, as though he were a second Sir Henry Taylor. Trollope gives this young man, in the same circumstances as he once went through, essentially a *happy* youth.

It isn't a particularly good book, though Trollope in old age obstinately insisted that it was: but, warmed by what had now accrued to him, he was trying to soften the memories of twenty years before.

TO PARSONS GAVE UP, WHAT WAS MEANT FOR MANKIND.

11
TIMETABLE

Success, when it did come, was sudden and complete. Within three years of the publication of *Barchester Towers*, he was one of the most popular novelists in England. He was a distinguished figure at the Post Office. He was chief of the surveyors, in charge of the eastern district, a senior member of the Post Office hierarchy. He had acquired a handsome country house in Essex. He was living the extraordinary organized life which he kept to for many years. He was presenting the face to the world by which his contemporaries knew him, a simple, decent, eccentric, mildly comic face. He was pleased that they should know him so. It wasn't how he knew himself. Nor should we, having the advantage, of course, of information denied to them.

There aren't, and weren't at the time, any secrets about the routine of his life. His acquaintances found it funny and at the same time slightly awesome. We can share in that. A good many great Victorians were restless with an energy that we seem to have lost. Dickens was a fantastically energetic man. So was Charles Kingsley. It may not have come quite so naturally to Trollope, but he had trained himself to habits of obsessive work – and obsessive play – even more demanding than Dickens's or Kingsley's.

His Essex house was at Waltham Cross, not far from the present railway line Liverpool Street–Bishop Stortford–Cambridge. It was a solid comely early-Georgian house and there, to some appearances, he could live like an East Anglian squire. That was pleasant, for he had a soft spot for squires, much more than for aristocrats or the up-and-coming rich. But no squire had ever spent his days like this.

He was wakened each morning at five. Five a.m. in an English winter is not an especially comfortable time. The lighting in rural Essex in the 1860s was not our lighting; there were candles, oil lamps, possibly gas. There was no heating but coal fires, and it was a big house. Of course, anyone like Trollope wouldn't mind or even notice those incidental features. What you are used to is all there is.

He was brought up a cup of coffee. At five-thirty a.m. he had settled down to his desk. He read through the work of the day before, and corrected it. By six he was writing. He wrote until nine-thirty. There was a watch in front of him. He had disciplined himself to write two hundred and fifty words each quarter of an hour. Thus the normal day's work would be two thousand five hundred words, though, even with Trollope, there were small fluctuations. He was marvellously concentrated, he could hold stories in his head as concretely as any writer of any time, but he wasn't a machine.

From this process emerged some of the best novels in English, *Framley*

Waltham House. 'In December 1859 . . . I settled myself at a residence about twelve miles from London, in Hertfordshire . . . which was somewhat too grandly called Waltham House.'
Autobiography

Parsonage, Orley Farm, The Small House at Allington, The Last Chronicle of Barset, Can You Forgive Her?, all written in the sixties according to that routine. This was the working timetable throughout the eleven years at Waltham House (1859–71). When, in the same period he was on his travels, on trains or shipboard, he managed to squeeze in a similar number of hours.[1]

At nine-thirty at Waltham he dressed for breakfast, a substantial English breakfast, meat, ham, fish, kidneys, eggs, bacon. However, though their meals were heavier than ours, they ate less often. This was his only genuine meal before the evening's dinner.

Breakfast over, he got down to the day's official work. Most of this was done in the eastern counties. If he had to go to headquarters, he arrived at St Martin's-le-Grand about eleven-thirty. This wasn't unusually late for a senior official. Up to 1939 high civil servants came late to their offices, and stayed late at the end of the day. Once at the Post Office, he worked with his usual speed and efficiency. There were diversions in the shape of arguments with the Secretary, Sir Rowland Hill, originator of the penny post, whom he couldn't bear. These were soothed down by his brother-in-law, John Tilley, by now the Assistant Secretary, an admirable civil servant.

Anyway, those commotions didn't matter. Trollope had become an institution, and reluctantly Hill and other administrators had to recognize his value. If he was a blustering nuisance in committee (there is fairly substantial evidence that he was, but all from Hill's supporters, such as Edmund Yates),[2] that had to be endured. No one could pretend that he wasn't knowledgeable or obsessively conscientious. If he did insist on writing novels – in which they may have taken a kind of

Forty-three Members in the Billiard Room of the Garrick Club, by H. O'Neil, 1869. The painting today hangs in the billiard room of the Garrick Club. Trollope is fourth from the left in the top row; Millais is on the extreme right holding a cue

ambivalent pride – it didn't make him less industrious as a public servant. Apparently no one complained.

No one complained, even, when he also insisted on hunting two days a week. That must have been rather more unusual for a senior official than literary activities.

On an ordinary non-hunting day, Trollope worked straight through till tea-time, about five p.m., when he arrived at his beloved Garrick Club. He says with resignation, and more than that:

> I have long been aware of a certain weakness in my character, which I may call a craving for love. I have ever had a wish to be liked by those around me – a wish that during the first half of my life was never gratified . . . The Garrick Club was the first assembly of men at which I felt myself to be popular.[3]

That was written of himself at the age of forty-six. At the club, secure at last, he settled down to a cup of tea and a rubber of whist. Tea, at that

Left A hunt breakfast. One of a set of six paintings entitled Bachelor's Hall, by F. C. Turner, 1835. Right Taking a Fence, by E. B. Herberte, 1881. 'When I first came to Waltham Cross in the winter of 1859–60, I had almost made up my mind that my hunting was over . . . As, however, the money came in, I very quickly fell back into my old habits.' Autobiography

time in the afternoon, was a fairly recent innovation. There is a minor trap here for readers of early Victorian novels. Tea, as a daily function, usually means a kind of nightcap, taken some hours after dinner, say between nine and ten, often with a miniature snack.

Whist over, he didn't stay for dinner with his friends at the Garrick. Back to Essex and his own table, finishing the day as a squire again. Plenty of guests, for he was entertaining lavishly now. Good and plentiful food, excellent wine.[4] Trollope himself was not a heavy drinker (by and large nineteenth-century writers drank much less than their successors)[5] but he was hearty and enjoyed himself. A cheeky woman once noticed at dinner that he partook largely of every dish offered to him. 'You seem to have a very good appetite, Mr Trollope.' 'Not at all, madam,' he replied, 'but, thank God, I am very greedy.'[6]

There is no record of the time he went to bed. Since he was going to get up day in, day out, at five, one hopes that it was pretty early.

His own self-mocking account of his writing procedure did him, as we all know, considerable harm with silly people. Books oughtn't to be written like that, they thought. Books *can't* be written like that. No proper writer can be so methodical. No proper writer can write so fast. These are the revelations of a wretched mercenary hack.

Almost all of that is, in the worst sense, vulgar. It also shows an inexcusable ignorance of literary history. First, it doesn't count at all how a work of art is composed. All that does count is the final result. Second, writing novels is a protracted operation, and all professional novelists by sheer necessity have had to be reasonably methodical – and this applies to steady citizens like Walter Scott down to intermittent alcoholics such as Faulkner and Fitzgerald. Third, many of the great novels of the world have been written faster than anything Trollope ever did. There is no rule. The *Chartreuse de Parme*, an enormously long book, was written in five weeks at three times Trollope's pace. *The Brothers Karamazov* was dashed off in apparent frenzy (though, of course, all such novels had been brooded on subterraneanly for long enough, which was also true of Trollope's best work). So were Dickens's early books dashed off: it became harder going later. So was the whole of Lawrence's corpus.

Balzac and Tolstoi did a lot of revision – Balzac on the proofs, which method would ruin a modern publisher – but *Les Grandes Illusions* and *War and Peace* were written at a rate that most writers passionately envy. So, perhaps surprisingly, was *A la Recherche du Temps Perdu* – also much revised in proof. It is much harder to think of a great novel written slowly, though there are a few.

Trollope's emergence as a novelist with a household name was convincing and dramatic. It had started through the circulating libraries. It was clinched by the shrewdness of George Smith, most brilliant of nineteenth-century publishers, and by the acquiescence and benevolence (and also the laziness) of Thackeray. *Doctor Thorne*, the third of the Barsetshire novels, had done much better than the first two. In a modest sense, Trollope was now established.

In the same modest sense, he wrote to Thackeray, whom he hadn't met, suggesting that he might be a possible contributor to the *Cornhill*.[7] The *Cornhill*, with Thackeray as editor, was shortly to be publishing its first number. George Smith, the proprietor and publisher, had already been offering terms to Trollope. All such magazines needed a novel in serial parts as the leading attraction – at the front of each issue. Thackeray didn't feel like exerting himself enough to produce anything substantial. George Smith proposed Trollope to fill the gap. Thackeray had read *The Three Clerks*, and approved. He wrote Trollope a letter of characteristic feline charm.[8] Trollope got to work at what to any other serious novelist who has ever lived, except Dostoevsky when pressed for money,[9] would have been impracticably short notice.

[91]

This was Trollope's decisive chance. He saw it and took it. This type of serial publication reached a much wider public than the normal three-volume work at thirty-one and six. The *Cornhill* was likely to be read, or at least appear on the tables, in a large proportion of educated homes.

Its circulation fluctuated somewhere round a hundred thousand a month. (Few novels in three volumes sold more than one-tenth of that.) Trollope had the personages and developments of future Barsetshire novels running through his mind. For anyone of his discipline it wasn't much of a strain, though it did mean an effort of physical endurance, to sit down to number four of the series and deliver the first instalment in time.

George Smith (right), *by G. F. Watts, 1876. At a banquet given by Smith for the contributors of his magazines, the* Cornhill *and the* Pall Mall Gazette, *Trollope first met Thackeray, G. H. Lewes, Richard Monkton Milnes* (left) *and Millais*

This happened at the end of 1859, just as the Trollopes were moving into Waltham House. That might have put other men off. It would have taken civil war in Essex to put Trollope off, and his chief reaction seems to have been that Waltham (which gave him the satisfaction of a New Place) was a lucky house.

Number four of the Barsetshire novels was *Framley Parsonage*. From the first number it was a scintillating success of a different order from anything before. The *Cornhill* had a marvellous start. Thackeray became an intimate friend, Trollope always admiring, though to do

Thackeray justice that wasn't the whole of their relation. He knew a good man when he saw one. George Smith, with his impresario's talent became another friend and handled Trollope with beautiful dexterity. Trollope became admired and loved by readers, a personality in literary London. It did a great deal for him. He says, with unusual gratification:

> I have certainly always had also before my eyes the charms of reputation. Over and above the money view of the question, I wished from the beginning to be something more than a clerk in the Post Office. To be known as some-body – to be Anthony Trollope if it be no more – is to me much. The feeling is a very general one, and I think beneficial.[10]

Left *Sir William Henry Gregory, a close friend of Trollope's at this time, was a contemporary at Harrow, and often entertained him at his country house, Coole Park, when Trollope first went to Ireland.* Right *Trollope as caricatured by Spy, 1873*

[93]

The success of *Framley Parsonage* seemed natural at the time, and does so now. It is lighter in tone than his greatest novels, but tells us a good deal. It contains some of his most accomplished feats of ethical conjuring (compare chapters 9–10 and 42 for Trollope's play with situation ethics). It doesn't explore people to the depth that he sometimes reached, but he himself considered, and many would agree, that Lucy Robarts is the best and most sparkling of his 'good' young women[11].

He was paid a thousand pounds for *Framley Parsonage*. This was the sale of the copyright entire, which was the contemporary custom and, with minor modifications, the one he adhered to throughout his career. Only about ten per cent of his lifetime earnings came from re-issues, subsidiary rights and the rest. A thousand pounds was twice as much as he had previously received for a novel, and for fifteen years or so his market price went steeply up, though the curve was dipping towards the end of his life.

So that after *Framley Parsonage* he was a distinctly prosperous writer. His average income during the eleven years at Waltham – Civil Service salary included, until he resigned towards the end of the period – was four thousand five hundred per annum. This was large for a professional writer and would be equivalent to at least fifty thousand today, perhaps more, since Trollope had to pay little income tax. However, it is desirable to get his financial success into proportion. He made nothing like the money Dickens did. In the 1860s Wilkie Collins was receiving appreciably more per book: for *Armadale* Collins was paid five thousand by the *Cornhill*, a figure that Trollope never achieved. Trollope reached a comfortable commercial plateau, but not the Victorian heights.

It was partly this which led him to the most fatuous resolution any major novelist ever made. He says, after the publication of *Doctor Thorne*: 'I was moved now by a determination to excel, if not in quality, at any rate in quantity.' The trouble was, Trollope's determinations were obstinately carried out. What happened in his will and the front of his head fortunately didn't interfere with the artist somewhere at the back, who was continuously brooding about his best work. But his will did compel him to a certain amount of folly.

12

THE GOLDEN TIME

This was Trollope's golden time, though three of his best books came later. He bought Waltham House in 1859 and left it in 1871. During those years he completed his Barset books with *Framley Parsonage, The Small House at Allington*, and the *Last Chronicle of Barset*: began the Palliser novels with *Can You Forgive Her?* and *Phineas Finn*: wrote good or goodish novels such as *Orley Farm, Rachel Ray, Miss Mackenzie, The Belton Estate, The Claverings, He Knew He Was Right, The Vicar of Bullhampton*: wrote bad or indifferent novels such as *The Bertrams, Castle Richmond, Ralph the Heir, Sir Harry Hotspur of Humblethwaite*: perpetrated idiocy with *The Struggles of Brown, Jones and Robinson* and a silly gesture with *Nina Balatka* and *Linda Tressel*.

It is possible to argue that even the indifferent books have flashes of Trollopian wisdom and Trollopian insight which occur nowhere else, and of which, without this flood of production, we should have been deprived. In terms of the tactics of literary reputation, in his own lifetime and later, it was a mistake to publish so much. In purer terms it may not have been. It is also true that nearly all major novelists who have lived into middle age have written plenty of books. The only clear exception is, curiously enough, Tolstoi.[1]

It would take greater ingenuity than that, however, to justify one of his productions. Trollope fancied himself as an uproarious humorist. He must have roared with laughter as he wrote every page of *The Struggles of Brown, Jones and Robinson*. It ranks as one of the least funny books ever written. The strange, intricate interior of Trollope's mind seems even stranger when one reflects that this nonsense was written almost simultaneously with the delectable sly understated humour of the Lady Amelia-Augusta passages in *Doctor Thorne* – when Lady Amelia writes to her cousin Augusta a superb, kind and considerate letter pointing out that, in the interests of Augusta's social situation, she really ought not to marry Mr Gazebee. The letters in Trollope's novels are usually as brilliantly differentiated as his characters' speech idiom, and this is one of the best. Augusta is convinced. Some time later she and her mother hear with surprise that her cousin Lady Amelia has thought it proper to marry Mr Gazebee. There is no more facetiousness in this dead-pan exchange than in Jane Austen, whom Trollope idolized.

There is overwhelming facetiousness in *The Struggles of Brown, Jones and Robinson*. Trollope insisted on its being published. George Smith, who knew all about the frailties of sensible men and of Trollope's in particular, humoured him and bought it for the *Cornhill*. Trollope says, wryly but still obstinate, nearly twenty years later: 'It was meant to be funny, was full of slang, was intended to be a satire on the ways of trade. Still I think there is some good fun in it, but I have heard no one else express such an opinion.'[2]

His other bizarre misdirection was to decide that he ought to publish some novels anonymously. This wasn't in search of money, which was his own explication of some of his overproduction. It was in fact the reverse of mercenary, a curious piece of quixotry.[3] At the height of his reputation and earning power, he had qualms. How much of all these rewards depended on his name alone? No other writer known to man has had this particular attack of conscience. Trollope being Trollope, he promptly acted on it. He wrote three shortish novels – *Nina Balatka, Linda Tressel, The Golden Lion of Granpère* – all in two volumes instead of three, all set by another bizarre misjudgment in parts of Europe he scarcely knew. The first two were published anonymously by Black-wood. They fell disastrously flat. Trollope remained sure that they were good. The moral for him was that more consideration was owing to the chagrins and practical ill-fortunes of disappointed authors. No successful writer has had more feeling for the unlucky.

Right from the beginning of this period of incessant creativity (Trollope's working life was so divided that a linear chronology isn't workable) he filled in his spare time by producing travel books. That happened because of the Post Office. As has been mentioned, number one in the hierarchy was Sir Rowland Hill, who returned Trollope's hostility. Number three was Hill's brother Francis, who did the same. Number two was John Tilley, once Trollope's brother-in-law, now re-married, a calm and temperate friend until Trollope died. Whatever the high-level arguments, there emerged a shrewd official idea of Trollope's uses.

In 1858, just before the great breakthrough with the *Cornhill*, he was sent to the West Indies to execute the same kind of inspection and re-organization as he had once done in the west of England. Nothing suited

Opposite The Hatch Family (detail), by Eastman Johnson, 1871. Upper-class Boston thought Trollope's manners rather ill-bred, which would have infuriated him

him better. He had every gift for a good traveller except ease with languages – immense physical energy, stamina, curiosity about everything he saw, unusual lack of national or racial prejudice. He was also conscientious to the limit. He was in the West Indies to get the letters delivered and to save the Post Office money. There is a nice anecdote that, riding forty miles or so in great heat, he became saddle-sore. Time was expensive and not to be wasted. He had to ride another forty miles next day. There was nothing for it. He sent for bottles of brandy, poured them into a basin, and into the basin descended a firm Victorian backside.[4]

Out of these experiences he wrote one of the most splendid travel books of the nineteenth century, still worth reading.[5] Then the Post Office had another idea. They decided that he might be an effective negotiator. Postal arrangements were still primitive, international undertakings were in the making. Contracts had to be settled. What about Trollope? To his acquaintances, Trollope as negotiator, impatient, noisy, argumentative, might have seemed a bad joke. Tilley must have known, and may have persuaded the Hills, that he was a good judge of men, and a good judge of hidden motives: and that, once set in the mode of duty, he would always be enduring, and could discipline himself to be patient.

At any rate, so it turned out. For the rest of his Post Office career, he became a star negotiator. Which led to more travel books, one on North America, also still worth reading,[6] though overladen with statistical data. He was in America at the beginning of the Civil War, and was far more sensible than most official Englishmen. He had no doubt that the North was bound to win, which was the opposite of contemporary English opinion. He had no doubt also that, on balance, theirs was the right side – again the opposite of contemporary English opinion. He had as keen a nose as anyone for corruption and incompetence, and there was plenty in the North. He thought that their military organization was contemptible, and admired the military virtues of the South. But he was unusually detached and free from romantic snobbery. In the long view the North must be in the right.

There couldn't have been many men more incessantly occupied than Trollope in the sixties. Working, travelling, the Post Office, living as the squire of Waltham – he revelled in it all, now that his taste of recognition had come. Whenever he was occupied, his spirits were high. This had always been true, which might seem a contradiction in one whose under-

Opposite *Florence: Piazza Santa Croce during Carneval* (detail), *by Giovanni Signorini. Before living in the Villino Trollope, Tom and Mrs Trollope had lived in the Via de Malcontenti next to Santa Croce*

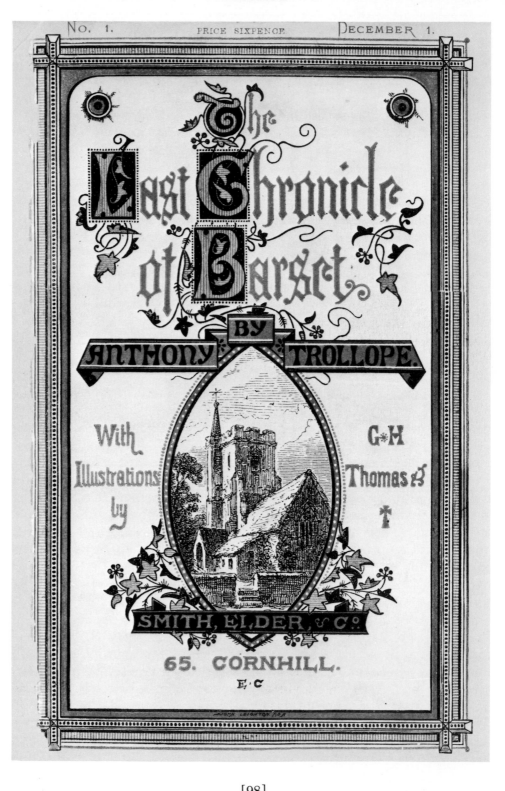

THE
CORNHILL MAGAZINE.

JANUARY, 1867.

The Claverings.

CHAPTER XXXIV.
MR. SAUL'S ABODE.

HEN Harry Clavering left London he was not well, though he did not care to tell himself that he was ill. But he had been so harassed by his position, was so ashamed of himself, and as yet so unable to see any escape from his misery, that he was sore with fatigue and almost worn out with trouble. On his arrival at the parsonage, his mother at once asked him if he was ill, and received his petulant denial with an ill-satisfied countenance. That there was something wrong between him and Florence she suspected, but at the present moment she was not disposed to inquire into that matter. Harry's love-affairs had for her a great interest, but Fanny's love-affairs at the present moment were paramount in her bosom. Fanny, indeed, had become very troublesome since Mr. Saul's visit to her father. On the evening of her conversation with her mother, and on the following

VOL. XV.—NO. 85.   1.

Opposite *Title page of* The Last Chronicle of Barset, *brought out in sixpenny monthly numbers in 1866–7. This method of publication was going out of fashion and on this occasion 'the enterprise was not altogether successful'. Trollope came to favour serialization in periodicals such as the* Cornhill (above): *the most popular novel the magazine was running always had pride of place on the first page*

tone was so melancholy: but in fact the states were linked, as they often are. One gets the feeling that immersing himself totally in whatever he was doing was a good therapy against the dark. He was almost certainly happier in this period than he had ever been before or was to be again. He had an unusual capacity for enjoyment, quite simple enjoyment, and sometimes not so simple.

[99]

It must have been pleasant to visit Tom and his mother in Italy, with his reputation made. That took place immediately after the success of *Framley Parsonage*, in the autumn of 1860, before his first American trip. There is no hint whether either Tom or Mrs Trollope accepted, admitted or even realized[7] that Trollope had become – suddenly, if seen from the outside – established as a major novelist. His mother anyway was too far gone to understand much, very old, happily retired from her literary treadmill, duty and effort no longer necessary, gently sozzling her last years away. As for Tom, Trollope had always respected and loved him, much more than the other way round. It was an asymmetrical relation, such as Trollope had in his early life regarded as his normal condition.

Even now, Tom was living in more luxurious state at the Villino Trollope in Florence than Trollope, for all his new prosperity, at Waltham House. Quite how this was managed is still something of a mystery. Living in Italy was, of course, cheap. But Tom's novels and articles can have brought him only very little, nothing like enough to sustain his life-style. The Villino became a main tourist attraction for English visitors to Italy. Dickens, who was intimate with Tom as he never was with Trollope, stayed there. So did the Leweses. So did a large slice of the English literary world: one met the Brownings, called on old Landor, basked in sybaritic holidays. Tom accordingly figures frequently in the mid-century memoirs of the travelled English. He is nearly always spoken of with affection, though at one time, as has been mentioned, Browning had his doubts about him and his mother. Tom impressed most people as the best natured of hosts, the perfect simple straight-forward Englishman.

Yet there is a suspicion that he had his devious side. He had married late, to a talented woman who was a singular mixture of Jewish, Indian and Anglo-Saxon. Theodosia had a little money which no doubt helped keep up the Villino. They had a child, Bice, after being married five years, which caused some gossip in the Anglo-Florentine colony. Then Tom's wife died, and left him three thousand pounds. He soon married again, to Frances Ternan, a sister of Dickens's mistress.[8] He continued to live much more lavishly than his brother, working away in Waltham and making his handsome income.

Tom collected pictures and *objets d'art*. There have been rumours that on the quiet he did a brisk trade as a dealer, using his social leadership

Opposite *Broadway, looking north from near Spring Street. Photograph by Mathew Brady, c. 1867. New York had been cleaned up since Dickens's 1842 visit, and Trollope enjoyed it – he detested Washington*

[100]

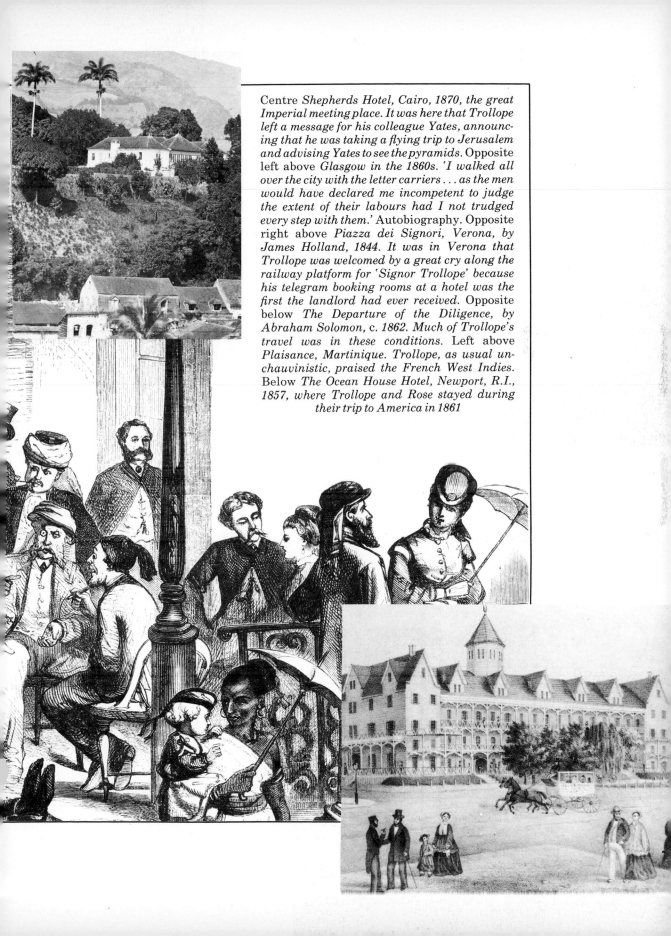

Centre *Shepherds Hotel, Cairo, 1870, the great Imperial meeting place.* It was here that Trollope left a message for his colleague Yates, announcing that he was taking a flying trip to Jerusalem and advising Yates to see the pyramids. Opposite left above *Glasgow in the 1860s.* 'I walked all over the city with the letter carriers . . . as the men would have declared me incompetent to judge the extent of their labours had I not trudged every step with them.' Autobiography. Opposite right above *Piazza dei Signori, Verona, by James Holland, 1844.* It was in Verona that Trollope was welcomed by a great cry along the railway platform for 'Signor Trollope' because his telegram booking rooms at a hotel was the first the landlord had ever received. Opposite below *The Departure of the Diligence, by Abraham Solomon, c. 1862.* Much of Trollope's travel was in these conditions. Left above *Plaisance, Martinique.* Trollope, as usual unchauvinistic, praised the French West Indies. Below *The Ocean House Hotel, Newport, R.I., 1857,* where Trollope and Rose stayed during their trip to America in 1861

Above *Mrs Trollope. She passed into amiable senility, and Trollope's reference to her death was matter-of-fact. Above right Theodosia, Tom Trollope's first wife. Anglo-Florentine society credited Theodosia with love affairs, but there is no real evidence. The Brownings were more interested in her than in Tom. Right Tom Trollope*

to impress American visitors.[9] It is an odd story. When one reads him, he sounds as incorruptible and rock honest as Trollope himself.

It was one of those American visitors, an American girl of just twenty-one, whom Trollope met on the mellow visit in 1860. Her name was Kate Field. This was the girl of whom he, usually so reticent, wrote the passage which has caused some speculation ever since. The passage has often been quoted but it is worth reading in full.

There is a woman of whom not to speak in a work purporting to be a memoir of my own life would be to omit all allusion to one of the chief pleasures which has graced my later years. In the last fifteen years [this was written in 1876] she has been, out of my family, my most chosen friend. She is a ray of light to me, from which I can always strike a spark by thinking of her. I do not know that I shall please her or do any good by naming her. But not to allude to her in these pages would amount to a falsehood. I could not write truly of myself without saying that such a friend had been vouchsafed to me. I trust she may live to read the words I have now written, and to wipe away a tear as she thinks of my feeling while I wrote them.[10]

Bice, the daughter of Tom's first marriage – attractive, talented, spoilt. She had a short marriage of considerable social lustre and died in childbirth

13
TROLLOPE'S ART: I

Trollope was a good and interesting man, but we should scarcely have heard of him (far less for instance than of Sir Henry Taylor) if he hadn't written his books. It is time to have a look at them.

Critics, in his own time and since, have never been comfortable with Trollope, and have tended to take refuge in a kind of patronizing unease. During his career, nearly forty years, there was a good deal written about him. There couldn't help being. After all, he wrote forty-seven novels, and Victorian magazines and journals, the *Spectator*, the *Saturday Review, The Times*, many others, had plenty of space. The reviewers were usually sensible and literate men. But they were puzzled.

These novels were, most of them, clearly enjoyable and possibly admirable: but why? They lacked 'imagination' – a quality, it seems, which the non-creative are always seeking to discover in the creative. He didn't transfigure life, which even his supporters, such as R.H. Hutton in the *Spectator*, felt that he ought to. They had a remarkable gift for missing his own most remarkable gift. It was only distinguished fellow-writers, Henry James, above all Tolstoi (who, unknown to the public and to Trollope himself, was a great admirer), who could identify that.

It is wrong, however, to think that in his lifetime he had a bad press. It was rather uncomprehending, and it was sometimes delivered from a lofty height. Dickens's books were usually received with an approach to idolatry. (There is a legend that Dickens once had a bad review and never looked at another. Quite untrue. Dickens took considerable satisfaction in good reviews and went to some trouble to secure them.) Thackeray got an amount of unqualified adulation not granted to Trollope. So did George Eliot. Nevertheless, most of the time Trollope received serious and on the whole affectionate attention. At the age of about sixty, when his fortunes were on the decline (compare chapter 17) he began to have definitely hostile criticism, as for *The Way We Live Now* and *The Prime Minister*.[1]

It is a nice irony of literary history that when the English critics were

A Private Box, by John Watkins Chapman, c. 1857. Such a party might have witnessed one of the six nights of Philip van Artevelde, *or Trollope's fictional performance of 'The Noble Jilt'*

being scornful about *The Prime Minister* (the entire press the worst he ever had for a serious novel, while modern opinion would rank it among his best) Tolstoi was overcome with enthusiasm for precisely the same book. 'Trollope kills me, kills me with his excellence.' Tolstoi was at that time writing *Anna Karenina*, and in the same correspondence there is a good deal of concern about 'the important thing'. That was the thing which will be mentioned soon. Tolstoi knew more about it than any writer.[2]

Even that period of disfavour for Trollope in England didn't last uninterrupted. There is a strong impression that his reputation was slipping precipitately years before his death. This was probably true in literary-intellectual circles, but it wasn't much reflected in the press. *The Duke's Children*, published at the age of sixty-five, attracted as much gratified praise (the note is always unmistakable, people can't disguise pleasure or the lack of it) as any of the books twenty years before. Which, incidentally, was entirely just.[3]

Throughout, the critics did their best, but they were puzzled as they had been in France about Balzac a generation before. As usual when puzzled, they produced a stereotype. Trollope was a photographer. It was a worthy thing to be, but not the highest. He could be respected for giving an exact replica of various sections of mid-century society, the clergy (that label clung to him right until death), the politicians, the aristocracy, the civil servants, the country gentry – a large slice, though not the whole, of the Victorian privileged world, roughly from the middle of the middle class up to the great landowners.

Well, that is true as far as it goes, or at least not demonstrably untrue.

A Cabinet council in Downing Street. The Duke of Omnium's Cabinet would have had a strong family resemblance

THE EARL OF CLARENDON   THE LORD CHANCELLOR   MR. CARDWELL   EARL DE GREY AND RIPON   MR. GLADSTONE   THE DUKE OF ARGYLL   MR. LOWE   MR. CHICHESTER FORTESCUE
   MR. JOHN BRIGHT   MR. CHILDERS   MR. BRUCE   LORD KIMBERLEY   LORD HARTINGTON   EARL GRANVILLE
   MR. GOSCHEN

He was an unusually exact and pertinacious observer. He had seen a great deal of that part of England, and was good at making the most of what he had seen. He had the kind of detached uncensorious temperament which was more interested in what he saw than in his own views of what it ought to be. He had a real gusto for what was. He had, that is, a sense of fact, and took delight in it. To an extent, though a misleading extent, he, like Archdeacon Grantly, enjoyed the worldliness of the world.

He would have done that wherever and whenever he was put down. He would have relished the toings and froings of a Unitarian chapel just as much as Barchester Cathedral, if that had happened to come his way. To use a grandiloquent old phrase, he had a passion for the physiognomic charm of phenomena.

But he didn't need to observe like a private detective. There the critics mistook the nature of the imagination which they thought he lacked. The Civil Service he knew, of course, at first hand, and his accounts are the most accurate we have. His direct experience of politics, though he came to know secondary politicians like Sir Henry James (not to be confused with Trollope's most scrupulous nineteenth-century critic) pretty well, was limited to being an unsuccessful Liberal candidate for Beverley. That doesn't prevent his studies of the human political process – as opposed to his sketches of political ideas, in which he wasn't much interested – being, according to the shrewdest modern parliamentarians, right both in tone and detail.[4]

The same with the church, though, as has been mentioned, he made one or two administrative slips. And the same with the pattern of living in the great ducal houses, so we are told by those who grew up in them[5]: though Trollope himself can, at the very best, have had only an occasional visit there (there is little evidence even of that), and a visit, if it ever happened, when he was famous and had already written exactly how the Pallisers lived in such a house.

So we can take it that here are precise records of human beings moving about in many layers of society, *circa* 1850–80. They are the most precise records extant. But, if he was a photographer, he was a very odd one – because, as we have just seen, he often didn't have much acquaintance with the object photographed.

Still, he wouldn't have minded the description. He knew, better than anyone, that this social representation was a minor, though an essential part of what he was trying to do. But he was both a modest and a realistic man. 'To be known as somebody – to be Anthony Trollope if it be no more' – was the limit of his expectation. If people in his own time knew him as a social photographer, that was better than nothing. A writer like himself was lucky to be known for a tiny part of his intention. He would probably have been overjoyed and astonished if he could have known that a hundred years later he was still known as a social photographer. For that does remain – and may remain so, despite the efforts of brilliant young American critics, until readers acquire extra intuition – a major part of his reputation.

In his modest fashion, he wouldn't have been surprised at that. He had been used to it in his own day. But he might have been surprised that this social photography, for which he is still being read and even cherished, is being surrounded by such an aura of nostalgia. Mid-Victorian England among Trollope's personages may seem desirable to us. It didn't seem specially so to them. Trollope was a much more acceptant man than Dickens, but he didn't like it overmuch, no more and no less than he would have liked any other period.

By and large, Victorians of his kind weren't overgiven to nostalgia, certainly not for recent historical periods. For instance, they didn't care for the eighteenth century in the sense we hanker after the nineteenth. They may have had more realistic historical memories or oral traditions. So far as they were nostalgic at all, it was for bogus Englands much further back. Trollope, for example, had a suppressed longing for the life of Saxon thanes surviving in their own land after the Conquest, living what he imagined to be an idyllic existence as medieval country gentlemen, their descendants represented lovingly in Trollope's novels by such families as the Thornes of Ullathorne. He wasn't for once inexact, he was just letting a romantic fancy run away with him.

Social representation, then, is the outer layer of Trollope's art. It is easy to recognize, and his readers did so from the beginning. They also felt a gratification at being let inside social groups, usually privileged and secretive social groups unknown to outsiders. Not many mid-Victorians had much idea of how people behaved inside a cathedral close, though the established church still had its hold on the country. They were quite ignorant about the Civil Service. They read the great speeches in parliament, but couldn't guess how those lofty figures talked to one another. So they took Trollope on trust – as it happened, rightly.

It was this aspect of Trollope that Nathaniel Hawthorne wrote about in a letter to Joseph M. Field, an American actor-manager (who, by a beautiful coincidence, was the father of the girl Trollope loved). The reference is well known, but it is worth noting, not only for what it says so generously, but also for what it leaves out.

> It is odd enough that my own individual taste is for quite another class of works than those which I myself am able to write . . . Have you ever read the works of Anthony Trollope? They precisely suit my taste – solid and substantial, written on the strength of beef and through the inspiration of ale, and

just as real as if some giant had hewn a great lump out of the earth, put it under a glass case, with all its inhabitants going about their daily business, and not suspecting that they were being made a show of.[6]

Of course, human beings live in society and are incomprehensible unless we understand it. But that is a platitude. We have to move another couple of layers inward before we come to what, as Trollope knew better than anyone, was his specific talent, his preoccupation and passion. Society, or a fraction of society, was useful to him on the way towards the central point, because human beings have to make choices and those choices are sometimes uniquely their own – in their freedom as the existentialists used to say – but more often conditioned by what society makes them do.

Trollope plays some marvellous moral and psychological conjuring tricks with these various kinds of choice – think of the old Warden, caught in an ingenious moral-social dilemma, or of Glencora, hesitating about running off with the man she loved, in essence though not appearance a purely human choice (where, despite Henry James, who wasn't rooted enough in sex to be infallible, she really could only choose one way), or Doctor Wortle, not certain how to treat justly a couple who by accident weren't married.

This layer of Trollope has recently become well recognized, and will be mentioned again in chapter 18. He had a delicate taste in the ethics of cases or, as one now says, situation ethics. It emerges in the autobiography as part of the process of building his own character: though sometimes his natural suspiciousness and scepticism make him doubt whether even honest men made their choices as they liked to think they did.

At last we come to what he set out to do and what he knew he did supremely well. For once, he half throws away his humility and tells us so. Before he speaks for himself, and before that is complemented by a statement from Henry James, who understood this depth of Trollope more profoundly than any English-speaking writer in the nineteenth century, the present writer wishes to make his own opinion clear. There is no simple term for Trollope's greatest gift – without which he would be an entertaining minor novelist.

When one says that no writer has been a better natural psychologist, that is saying something but not enough. He could see each human being he was attending to from the outside as well as the inside, which is an essential part of the total gift. That is, he could see a person as others saw him: he could also see him as he saw himself. He had both insight and empathy, working together in exceptional harmony. Further, and this may be even more uncommon, he could not only see a person in the here-and-now, with immediate impact, but also in the past and in the future. That diachronic vision is of course developed by experience and is impossible without it: but one can have all the experience in the world and still be completely lacking in it. In Trollope, the capacity must have been latent very early. It is already developed in his first book. Natural psychologists are fairly rare, but not too rare. Natural psychologists who have both insight and foresight combined are very rare indeed.

For want of a better shorthand expression, let us call this human equipment of Trollope's *percipience*. How many people possess it, even to a limited degree, we just don't know. He possessed it to an abnormal degree, perhaps as high as anyone on record. Those who don't possess a shred of it not unnaturally don't see anything in him. It is like people who can see only in black and white being asked to recognize the colour blue.

On the other hand, people with more than the normal share of Trollopian percipience occur here and there in all kinds of places, often, and perhaps usually, right outside literary or aesthetic domains. Good priests, sometimes; doctors with an unusual diagnostic gift: some politicians who owe their survival to making the correct judgments of people round them: soldiers, ditto: sometimes people totally beaten by life, finding a fulfilment in being expert spectators. It may be more common in women than in men, and it may not be an accident that women often seem to understand Trollope's novels more naturally and deeply than men.

Trollope himself told us what he thought. The modesty drops away, as it should, when someone is certain, without assertion, that he knows exactly what he is talking about. He says:

> He [Trollope is speaking of himself as novelist] desires to make his readers so intimately acquainted with his characters that the creatures of his brain should be to them speaking, moving, living, human creatures. This he can never do, unless he knows these fictitious personages himself, and he can never know them unless he can live with them in the full reality of established intimacy. They must be with him as he lies down to sleep and as he wakes from his dreams. He must learn to hate them and love them. He must argue with them, quarrel with them, forgive them, and even submit to them. He must know of them whether they be cold-blooded or passionate, whether true

Opposite above *Trollope, by Samuel Laurence, 1865.* Opposite below *Thackeray, seated in The Garrick Club, by John Gilbert, 1864. 'I regard him as the most tender-hearted human being I ever knew, who, with an exaggerated contempt of the world at large, would entertain an almost equally exaggerated sympathy with the joys and troubles of individuals around him.*
Autobiography

[112]

or false, and how far true and how far false. The depth and the breadth and the narrowness and shallowness of each should be clear to him. And, as here, in our outer world, we know that men and women change, – become worse or better as temptation or conscience may guide them, – so should these creations of his change, and every change should be noted by him. On the last day of each month recorded, every person in his novel should be a month older than on the first. If the would-be novelist have aptitudes that way, all this will come to him without much struggle: but, if it do not come, I think he can only make novels of wood.

It is so that I have lived with my characters, and thence has come whatever success I have obtained. There is a gallery of them, and of all in that gallery I may say that I know the tone of the voice, and the colour of the hair, every flame of the eye, the very clothes they wear. Of each man I could assert whether he would have said these or the other words: of every woman, whether she would then have smiled or so have frowned. When I shall feel that this intimacy ceases, then I shall know that the old horse should be turned out to grass. That I shall feel it when I ought to feel it, I will by no means say. I do not know that I am at all wiser than Gil Blas's canon: but I do know that the power indicated is one without which the teller of tales cannot tell them to any good effect.[7]

Trollope wasn't much given to rhetoric, but he is encouraged into rhetoric in that passage. He was even less given to boasting, but here he is boasting. On this subject few men have had more right to boast.

Almost for the only time in his autobiography he is writing with unqualified confidence. In principle, perhaps not in detail (there are thousands of characters in the Trollope corpus, and he can't have known each one of them so perfectly), what he says is true. We can read the proof of it in the books. And the degree of obsessiveness is precisely what we should expect. It is perhaps essential, probably quite essential, to any kind of first-rate creative work. We have learned that from what so many of the greatest creative persons have told us, from Newton and Einstein downwards. The ability to keep the creative task obsessively in mind is one of the most cardinal of all abilities. Going to bed without being able to leave a fictional creation, nagging at how he could be made more truthful and living, isn't a rhetorical flourish. Trollope had done that.

It is necessary for anyone who is trying to reach a truth. In some of his characters, Trollope did reach a truth. That sounds a disparaging tribute. It isn't. There are very few novelists of whom it ought to be said. It was the reason why Tolstoi admired him so much. This was the im-

Opposite *The Preston By-Election* (detail), *by W. P. Sherwood, 1868. The year that Trollope stood unsuccessfully as candidate for Beverley in Yorkshire*

Left *Yes, by Sir John Everett Millais, 1877. With the air of melancholy suitable for Alice Vavasour at last, and for the second time, accepting John Grey.* Right *Come In, by Charles Green, 1877. The interruption is not frustrating as it was when Plantagenet Palliser was distracted from his quints*

portant thing. Obviously Tolstoi would have been a great writer if, as part of his art, he hadn't had the identical purpose. Trollope would not have been a great writer without it. But it was enough.

There is an acute comment in Henry James' major essay on Trollope. This was written when James was forty,[8] confident of his own gift. He had always enjoyed Trollope, but as a young man had had all an aesthete's reservations. Anyway, Trollope is too difficult a writer for young men, even if they are as clever as Henry James.

In maturity James had developed some of his own percipience. He wrote, in the middle of a long essay, searching with Jamesian scrupulous anxiety to discover at last why Trollope actually was so good:

> If he was in any degree a man of genius (and I hold that he was) it was in virtue of this happy, instinctive perception of human varieties. His knowledge of the stuff we are made of, his observation of the common behaviour

[114]

of men and women, was not reasoned or acquired, not even particularly studied. All human beings deeply interested him, human life, to his mind, was a perpetual story: but he never attempted to take the so-called scientific view, the view which has lately found ingenious advocates among the countrymen and successors of Balzac.[9] He had no airs of being able to tell you *why* people in a given situation would conduct themselves in a particular way: it was enough for him that he felt their feelings and struck the right note, because he had, as it were, a good ear. If he was a knowing psychologist he was so by grace; he was just and true without apparatus and without effort... We care what happens to people only in proportion as we know what people are. Trollope's great apprehension of the real, which was what made him so interesting, came to him through his desire to satisfy us on this point – to tell us what certain people were and what they did in consequence of being so.

Right at the end of this examination – in which, as so often with James, conscience, taste and instinct aren't completely in unison – he finishes:

Trollope will remain one of the most trustworthy, though not one of the most eloquent, of the writers who have helped the heart of man to know itself.

There aren't many better statements about Trollope's percipience or the meaning of the realistic novel. Trollope never read that. It was written soon after his death, and published, in its final form, five years later. However, Trollope had written just one more boast, though a muted one, in the autobiography.

I do not think it probable that my name will remain among those who in the next century will be known as the writers of English prose fiction: but if it does, that permanence of success will probably rest on the characters of Plantagenet Palliser, Lady Glencora and the Reverend Mr Crawley.[10]

He wasn't at all a good judge of his novels as a whole, but on this he was on his home ground. Those three still seem, to readers in 1975, the height of his percipience. Others, such as Archdeacon Grantly, show at least as much projective power. Lucy Robarts is as good as Glencora, but without as much scope to display herself. For anyone who can take percipience at its least hopeful, Lady Mabel Grex is one of the best women in fiction.

It was his triumph to tell the truth about those characters and still leave them embossed in our experience. Both he and James would have agreed that some other characters in fiction, seen with visions not realistic, quite different from the Trollope percipient vision, have travelled further and will probably last longer – Don Quixote, Micawber, Sarah Gamp, Sherlock Holmes. But such figures depend on leaving things out – just as sentimentality does. The full truth about human beings depends on not leaving things out: and that is usually too difficult for our simple stereotype-attracted minds. It was Trollope's feat to tell so much of the truth about his great characters. There, not elsewhere, he achieved one of the peaks of realistic novel writing.

It was possible only, as James said and has been suggested with a rather different emphasis here, through a natural and specific gift, probably one of the rarest gifts. Even so it wasn't as easy as it looked. He had to invent and discipline his own technical resources. These have their interest, in comparison with those of others, and may bear a little inspection later on.[11]

Lord Lufton and Lucy Roberts. Illustration from Framley Parsonage, *by Sir John Everett Millais. At the beginning of their relation, but she wouldn't have been quite so gloomy*

14
A HUMAN RELATION

I

When Trollope couldn't resist sending that final message to the unnamed woman, he meant no less and no more than what he said. Kate Field, and perhaps even more the idea of Kate Field, had brightened his existence. She came into it just at the beginning of his decade of maximum fortune – the sixties. She never quite faded out until he died. Astonishingly, there was no pain at any time on either side. It was a relation which brought him a singular kind of happiness, though it wouldn't have done to other men. She gave him precisely what he wanted: and he may have done the same to her.

The concrete facts are obvious enough. He loved her. He never went to bed with her. The evidence is reasonably conclusive that Kate Field never went to bed with anyone in her life, though a good many men, and some women, would have liked the chance.[1] She had great charm, good looks, intelligence and spirit, but like Trollope she was much less coherent and adjusted than she seemed. The ending of one of his letters sets the tone of the relation:

> Give my kindest love to your mother. The same to yourself, dear Kate, – if I do not see you again [i.e. in America, which he had been visiting] – with a kiss that shall be semi-paternal, one-third brotherly and as regards the small remainder, as loving as you please.[2]

Trollope could have had his amorous successes, if he had let himself go. He had the kind of subtlety of temperament which would have appealed to women as clever as himself. But he was diffident: also he had a good marriage, and he was bound to the morality of his times. It is as certain as such things can be that he never consciously contemplated trying to make love to Kate. It is perhaps nearly as certain that occasionally his realistic daydreams formed themselves, and he imagined what might happen if his wife died.

[117]

In Florence, where they met, in Boston, Washington, New York, and in London later, he and Kate can't have been alone together more than maybe a couple of dozen times. That wouldn't satisfy anyone in a conventional love affair. They wrote a lot of letters, of which his only have survived. It is possible to guess the feeling of some of hers from his replies, but those missing letters, along with his wife's, are the part of Trollope correspondence which might tell us most about him. His are delightful. The bluff, over-simple façade breaks down altogether. He is funny, devious, acute, protective, loving (in a particular and revealing tone). He is, in fact, for the first and only time in his letters, the man who could have written the girl characters in his novels, and have loved them.

There is one interesting point. The correspondence dried up when there was no prospect of meeting, and started again as soon as there was. Trollope was, as by now should be clear, a deeply imaginative man. He must have been holding Kate in his imagination for a good many years. But he was also too practical to work in a vacuum, so to speak, as a younger man might have done. Perhaps even he occasionally felt he was writing enough words anyway, however much he loved thinking of this girl.

At their first meetings, in the Villino Trollope, on Florentine autumn nights, no doubt exhilarated by Tom's iced lemonade, Trollope felt all the simple responses, obtained the simple impression of Kate which those writing about him have cherished since. They were both happy.[3] Kate, air-borne with artistic aspirations, was being introduced to one of the most cultivated artistic societies in Europe, the Brownings, George Eliot and Lewes, the aged Landor. They were all making a fuss of her, particularly old Landor, who was paying her stately compliments and giving her presents.

While Trollope was at last, and really for the first time, being received as a major fellow-writer by the Brownings (Elizabeth wrote some slightly catty praise which he cheerfully coped with). Trollope personally revered George Eliot, and, though he had been friendly with her and Lewes for a couple of years, this was the start of an intimacy which endured all their lives. She read his novels aloud and learned from them,[4] he thought hers magnificent,[5] and he became something of a masculine support after Lewes – a very long way after. So all was good, more than good, for Trollope and Kate in the Villino garden.

It was conventional, particularly among her English friends, to say how beautiful Kate was. That wasn't really true. American journalists, who were better judges, decided later that she wasn't beautiful nor per-

Opposite *Kate Field*

[118]

haps in the ordinary sense pretty. What was more attractive, she had great awareness of her physical presence. She dressed with careful taste, like a cultivated rich young woman. She had grace. Trollope always had a special predilection for what he called low brown girls: which didn't mean debased Asiatics, but not-too-tall brunettes. Kate neatly met that specification. Incidentally, nearly all the literary dignitaries of those Florence parties, except the Trollope men and George Eliot, would seem diminutive by our standards, just as would Dickens, Collins, and all members of Lenin's pre-revolutionary committee.

It wasn't only Kate's looks which took Trollope by storm and almost immediately set him free. It took only a second meeting before his reserve was broken and he was starting to educate her (a time-worn procedure of a middle-aged man with an attractive girl). He was promising to send her books. He had not met anyone like this before. At that stage he is unlikely to have met any American women, and the manners of well brought up American women in the 1860s were different from those of their English contemporaries, and much more endearing. Kate was American enough to have no use for the prissiness, the coy silences, which had become the fashion in England (though we know from Trollope's heroines that all that was very much a façade).

But Kate in reality wasn't typical of American girls or any others. She was direct, in a way which must have been a treat to Trollope. She was ready to make the running. She wanted to launch into her own hopes,

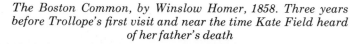

The Boston Common, by Winslow Homer, 1858. Three years before Trollope's first visit and near the time Kate Field heard of her father's death

dreams, plans, and took time off (there is no clear evidence of this, but Trollope, though not at all self-centred, must have wished to get in an occasional word about his own concerns) to draw him out about his. She met him, quickly, with the barriers of age, fame, nationality, all crashed away. She was naked to life, and expected him to be. She was an example of spiritual democracy, and assumed that they talked on equal terms. She moved into intimacy, or at least the first stage of intimacy, very quickly. She was highly intelligent, probably, apart from George Eliot and despite his wife's shrewdness, the most intelligent woman he had ever talked to.

She had many ideals, at some of which Trollope, even at the beginning, must have been secretly amused. She was, in a self-absorbed fashion, honest and kind. He was far too intuitive not to have seen that quite soon. Her conversations with Landor in his eighties are a model of how a clever alluring girl ought to flirt with and give pleasure to a very old man. Trollope was, of course, much too young and vigorous for any such playfulness, and she had enough sense not to try it.

That is the picture of Kate Field which has been redrawn by successions of Trollope students. Much of it is true as far as it goes, but it doesn't go anything like far enough. Kate wasn't just a simple, positive, desirable, rich American girl. It takes two to make a human relation of the curious kind she and Trollope sustained: it took an unusual woman to draw from Trollope, long after the first excitement had died away, his grateful cry from the heart. Kate wasn't just one of Ibsen's girls strayed into the wrong country. She wasn't even James' Isabel Archer in search of excellence. She was as interesting, and in many ways as complex, as Trollope himself.

Both her father and mother were actors and theatrical impresarios, though in a refined fashion superior to the public taste. With the result that they constantly lost money in the state of Missouri. They had some New England connections, and one of Mrs Field's sisters had married a well-to-do Bostonian. So, though Kate's own family had no money, there was an air of money around. Kate was sent to good private schools, her aunt – only fourteen years older than Kate herself – paying the bills. Kate was a dazzling child, and some of that aura stuck with her always – beautifully groomed, nice to look at, top in all subjects (except algebra, abstract thought not being one of her skills). She was miscellaneously talented, and at fifteen was already wondering whether she ought to concentrate on literature, singing, or the stage.[6]

She was self-willed a long way beyond the ordinary, and her father, a sensitive and loving man, thought she was marvellous but worried about fatalities ahead. She and her young aunt were engrossed in a pure but intense affection. Several times in her life she evoked rapturous love in older women, and she to an extent responded, as with the Italian actress Ristori. The only connected account of her life was written by a woman more than half in love with her, and a good deal distorted on that account.

It is important to keep our heads and not classify her as a homosexual. The Victorians were much wiser than we are in that respect, and didn't separate sex as a special category set aside from all the rest of the emotional life. Trollope would, of course, have identified her aunt's passionate feeling and taken it in his stride. He was the last man to tag dismissive labels on to anyone. Anyone who doubts that should read the sub-text about Dean Arabin. Like a good many of the clever young men intoxicated by the Oxford Movement, Arabin had a long stretch of exalted male friendships – or loves, to call them by their proper name. Present-day observers would have categorized him as a homosexual, and settled him for good and all. Trollope had too much comprehensive sense for that (and so had other mid-Victorians, as is shown in the novels of Dickens, George Eliot, Wilkie Collins).

When Kate had just turned seventeen, her father died. This was a profound shock. In spite of financial upheavals, the home was stable and gently loving. She was a self-regarding girl, but hadn't lost her dependence on both parents, father above all. Now he had left her with a void in her existence – and, as a minor consequence, nothing but debts. Kate went for an Italian sojourn on her aunt's money – or more accurately on her uncle-in-law's. She gave the impression of being a well-endowed young woman, and hadn't a dollar of her own.

She also went to Italy longing for a father. As a rule, slick diagnoses are to be avoided, but perhaps this one does help a little. She was charming with many people, most of all with aging men – very old ones like Landor, also men round her father's age, not only Trollope but his brother Tom, Browning, later on Dickens. She was specially charming, of course, because her heart was in it.

At first sight, and for a long time afterwards, Trollope made a most adequate father-surrogate. And she made a more than adequate daughter-cum-love. He soon knew her very well, which was child's play to him, though loving child's play. Her egotism, her wilfulness, her strong will, her raving ambition, her lack of run-of-the-mill prudence – it didn't need his intuition to discover all that in the midst of what, though it sounds insipid, was a curious pervading sweetness.

II

Trollope took delight in guiding her. He gave her advice, tried to keep her in order, used all his wisdom, fell into an idiom at the same time disciplinary and tender (which was naturally in a subdued sense amorous, and probably tells something of what he would have been like in an active love). He enjoyed himself. We don't know how she replied, either face to face or in her letters, but the only reasonable assumption is that she enjoyed herself too.

She stood up to him, that is obvious. The bones of her character, even in her early twenties, were already showing through. She probably teased him, being witty but not specially humorous. She was enough of a normal young woman to like being petted by a distinguished man. As we shall see in a moment, she showed him – which wasn't so true of her in later life – a special kind of tact, gentleness, or consideration. There

Kate Field

were some issues, pleasing to us spectators after a hundred years, flickering between them. As an agreeable start, Trollope's advice, given with devoted attention and all his knowledge, worldly and unworldly, wasn't particularly good. For almost the only time on record it was sometimes remarkably bad. Fortunately she didn't take it.

He was afraid that she would try to succeed in too many directions, and spray her talents away – a reasonable fear which would have occurred to most sensible men. In Florence she had been attempting to get her voice trained: simultaneously she was sending articles (quite good articles) to America on miscellaneous aesthetic topics. Trollope, born professional, didn't like to see her a dilettante. He had soon dis-

[123]

covered, of course, that her appearance of wealth was deceptive and that she would not only have to earn a living for herself, but also to keep her mother.

Further, on his first visit to America, a year after their meeting in Florence, he must also have discovered that she had sacrificed her chance of an inheritance. He saw more of her on that trip than at any other time. It was the beginning of the American Civil War. Trollope, as has been mentioned, was firmly on the Northern side. Kate, who was about as given to compromise as Joan of Arc, was purely and blazingly so. She was an idealist, she already had the fervour – and in Boston the beginnings of the appeal – of a public personality.

She made her opinions clearly known. Her uncle-in-law didn't approve. He was a conservative wealthy man and like other conservative wealthy men in the north was frightened of any talk of abolition of slavery and equality for Negroes. Dangerous talk. It was necessary to keep quiet. He had no children, and had been intending to leave his fortune to Kate. But, if she persisted with this campaigning or anything like it, he couldn't see his way to doing that. He would have to alter his will. It presented for Kate a nice Trollopian problem in the ethics of choice. But she wasn't the young woman to hesitate about such a choice. She persisted. She was duly disinherited.

This family ultimatum seems to have been discussed in a remarkably temperate manner. Kate remained attached to her young aunt (it isn't unlikely that her aunt's husband didn't entirely care for that attachment), and aunt and husband continued to help her out with small loans, which Kate conscientiously paid back. Nevertheless, her expectations had vanished. Her mother depended on her. She had to make money immediately for the two of them.

It was here that Trollope's advice was curiously wrong. He wanted her to settle down, and discipline herself to serious writing. No one alive knew the profession of letters better than he did. If he had been less enraptured, he would have been more judicious. She had a little literary talent, but not the patience or stamina to work away for years. Incidentally she couldn't afford to. She was quite a good journalist, which contributed to her income for the rest of her life. A century later, she might have become a star woman columnist.

What she really wanted to do was something more conspicuous. Quite early, in her middle twenties, she aimed to become a famous lecturer. Lecturers in mid-century America were as it were the television celebrities of their day. Kate liked the idea. She believed she could make an impact. She did. Before she was forty, she was one of the best known women in the country and had acquired a reputation, a handsome income, and a packet of shares in the new Bell Telephone Company, a gift whose value multiplied by forty under her eyes and left her comfortably off.

When she revealed this plan to Trollope, long before she had appeared on a platform, he protested. He was himself without any histrionic streak. He was a poorish speaker and a bad public performer. He didn't care for people like Dickens who loved showing off and were supremely

Trollope in his mid-sixties

good at it. He probably was uncomfortable with the exhibitionist impulses in Kate, and suspected they would do her harm.

In a sense, this was true – but, like a man in love, he wanted her to be a more normal woman than her nature would let her. In another sense, just as he over-estimated her literary talent, he under-estimated her daimon. He didn't accept that she was as ambitious as he had once been, and that she had a much stronger ego and more steely will. She wasn't a wise young woman, and didn't become wiser with age. Trollope was the wisest man she had met, or was likely to meet. But about what was

[125]

necessary for her, she was right. It was an irony, which, in a detached mood, Trollope would have enjoyed.

He wouldn't have enjoyed another, though it does her credit. It seems to have escaped most Trollopian commentators, but the evidence is definite and well documented.[7] All through her first intimacy with Trollope she was in love with another man, or at least believed she was.

This she didn't betray to Trollope, not by so much as a hint, not even when he was lovingly probing. This may have been partially, of course, because she didn't want to lose him. Kate was a pure soul, but she had her share of ordinary rapacity. The evidence suggests that wasn't the main reason. She certainly let Trollope think, and he wasn't an easy man to deceive, that she had a kind of love for him. He makes this apparent, using the unambiguous word, in a letter.[8]

It is more likely that she had a feeling that the relation was more important to him than it was to her. She may have flattered herself about it. She had given him, perhaps puzzlingly to herself, a happiness which was evident whenever she saw him. She didn't want to break it. She may very well have had the casual good nature not uncommon in those who are emotionally ardent and sensually cold – which she almost certainly was. She would seem to most of us, not enraptured, a tiresome and opinionated girl, but she was fundamentally good in her feelings.

III

The man with whom she fell in love at twenty-one, was an American artist of her own age. He seems to have been totally incapable of making up his mind: in fact, he may have attracted her because neither of them really wanted serious love or marriage, nothing but an emotional parade. Still, he kept re-appearing, and eight years after they first met she wrote him a letter of singular rancour. She was not a rancorous woman but she didn't like being let down.

I have never seen the moment until now that I could sit down and tell you my opinion of you and your letter . . . The letter you wrote last December ought to have been written in 1862. You were a moral coward not to have written it then . . . By not writing that letter you made me fancy that I had allowed myself to be much more interested in you than you were in me . . . Your tardy letter assures me that I was not this idiot, and my regard for my own common sense is much greater than it has been for six years. I thank God that you did not remain longer in Florence, and that I did not tarry in Paris, for had you offered me your hand, I should have accepted it, believing you to be other than you are – and been cured. When my eyes open they open very wide. I am not one to submit tamely to wrong, and separation if not divorce would have been the inevitable consequence of such an ill-assorted union.[9]

This rings like a love affair in which vanity and pride are ruling motives, and in which both participants are using the imbroglio as a protection – that is, while they could go on quarrelling, they weren't in danger of an attachment more real.

If Rose Trollope had died, Kate would have been in danger of another attachment. Trollope would certainly have wanted to marry her. The likelihood is that she would have shilly-shallied and at last agreed. It might have worked for some time. She would have found him a stronger character than she took him for. But she was out of all comparison more self-bound than he was, and maybe 'separation if not divorce' would have darkened his old age.

Things were better as they were. It was an ethereal relation, but completely unshadowed. On her side the feeling peacefully diminished. As with others in whom the sensual impulses are weak, her affections and loves died away rather fast (this was so towards her once beloved aunt). In Trollope they didn't. The outburst about her in the autobiography was written sixteen years after he first met her, and the emotion runs as strong as ever.

People have wondered how Rose Trollope responded to that outburst. Almost certainly she knew in advance. Her son Henry was his father's literary executor and prepared the autobiography for publication. He was empowered to edit and make any deletions he thought proper. He made none, and wrote an introduction. If either he or Rose had qualms, nothing would have been simpler than to take out the Kate passage.

Rose was aware of all that had happened between Trollope and Kate. With her usual cool competence, she had behaved as though it was a good idea, became friendly with Kate herself,[10] and insisted on her staying in the house.

We don't need to sanctify Rose, but it is not inconceivable that she knew her husband better than we can, and was at least half glad that something of the kind had come his way. No doubt kind friends asked kind friendly questions about the unnamed woman in the autobiography. If Rose was as sharp-tongued as we might infer, she would have coped with that.

What did Kate give him, apart from happiness? A curious happiness which wouldn't have been so much of a joy to many men. She didn't affect his art, it was too profoundly formed and mature for that. His insight into young women was already at its deepest before he met her, and he had written about them as well as he was ever to do. There is no character in all his work of whom Kate is the sole origin. Yet, in a subtle pervasive fashion there are plenty of traces in the sub-text – not only in the theme of *An Old Man's Love*. In that book, the girl is nothing like Kate, but the feeling is very near the bone.

Isabel Boncassen in *The Duke's Children* is not much like Kate either, but with her one sometimes hears a clear, pleasantly imperious voice. It is easy to detect some American stresses which he had heard Kate use. Much more concealed, some of the longings for women's independence from *English* girls in the later novels lead back to his young woman. The English girls' existences are more sheltered, they aren't so formidable or self-willed, but sometimes the intensity shines out of them.

In the same way, the behaviour of both the Duke and Silverbridge to Isabel Boncassen shows two aspects of Trollope's first-hand response – the young man at a loss before a girl of spirit fiercer than his own (Trollope felt this with Kate, just as a young man would), the Duke moved by an emotion which wasn't entirely that of a decorous future father-in-law. A little detective work discovers many such private reminiscences, the sort of self-indulgence some writers allow themselves when they use a reference known only to themselves.

What Kate gave him most, though, was the confidence of intimacy. He talked and wrote to her as equal to equal, letting himself wander, mixing love messages with serious opinions, free as he seems to have been with no one else. There is a pleasant example in a letter of August 1862:

> My very dear Kate, I forget when I wrote to you last, I hope it was not very long ago, and that in writing now I display my own great merit rather than satisfy any just claim of yours. [He is writing from Waltham House, she is in Boston. The letter is long, and he comes to remarks of hers about his American travel book.] Your criticisms are in part just – in part unjust, in great part biased by your personal (– may I say love?) for the author . . . What am I to say about your present state? [i.e. that of the North] I am not myself so despondent, as it seems to me are many of you Yankees. Things will go worse before you gain your object than I thought they would; but still you will ultimately gain it. This conscription is very bad. Was it absolutely necessary? My feeling is that a man should die rather than be made a soldier against his will. One's country has no right to demand everything. There is much that is higher and better and greater than one's country. One is patriotic only because one is too small and too weak to be cosmopolitan . . . Tell me whom you see, socially, and what you are doing socially and as regards work, how little we often know in such respects of those we love dearest. Of what I am at home, you can have no idea; – not that I mean to imply that I am of those you love dearest. And yet I hope I am.[11]

That letter tells things about Trollope different from anything in his autobiography, and shows how fluid, under the character he had so conscientiously built, his personality still was.

15

RESIGNATION

Trollope lived in Waltham House from 1859 to 1871. Then, with the cautiousness of one who had known poverty and suffered from it, he thought that his prosperity, though not obviously sliding, might not last: and so, for economy's sake, gave the house up. It had brought him the booming years. This had been the time of nearly all his best-known books – although two of the finest were to come much later. During that time he had committed a step that added to his cautiousness about money. He had resigned from the Civil Service.

Michael Sadleir, and others who have followed him, have got this story perceptibly wrong.[1] The legend, started by Edmund Yates,[2] who had hidden resentments, is that Trollope resigned in an outburst of temper, having been passed over for promotion.

It is true that he was angry about being passed over. He says as much, straightforwardly and resentfully. It is almost the only sign of bitterness in the later part of his autobiography. He behaved with considerable lack of control at the time, and with singular stupidity, as official papers show. But there were well over two years between that event and his resignation, and Trollope's temper, though hot, didn't last that length of time. One really can't resign in a huff three years late. He was sad when he left the Post Office, but he left on good personal terms. It was a considered choice, though he later thought it might not have been a wise one.

It is now possible to reconstruct nearly all the story from Post Office records. Sir Rowland Hill retired from the Secretaryship at the office in the spring of 1864. Trollope and he, we know, actively disliked each other. Trollope makes this more than clear. To him, Hill was a cold, ungiving little man, with no spark of human warmth, utterly incapable of looking after human beings. Further, he had been brought in to govern the Post Office, through public and political pressure, from outside: and Trollope, who had a passionate institutional loyalty, couldn't forget this.

On his side, Hill undoubtedly felt that Trollope was offensively bois-

[129]

Left *Trollope, by R. Birch, after a photograph by Sarony.* Right
*Sir Rowland Hill. 'I was always an anti-Hillite, acknowledging,
indeed, the great thing Sir Rowland Hill had done for the
country, but believing him to be entirely unfit to manage men or
arrange labour.'* Autobiography

terous, quarrelsome, arrogant (which he seems to have been in official
dealings), prepared to use his external influence and literary reputation
to go over Hill's head to ministers. (The Postmaster General was usually
a not too prominent aristocrat such as Lord Elgin, the Duke of Mont-
rose, Lord Stanley of Alderley, and by the sixties they were all much
more likely to meet Trollope socially than the businesslike official Hill.)
Frederick Hill, the Junior Secretary (number three – the Post Office
terminology of the time is confusing, and different titles are used by
Trollope and others) was, in Trollope's view, like his brother only worse.
Frederick Hill shared his brother's view of Trollope, slightly more
bleakly.

Trollope had to struggle with his prejudices to recognize that Rowland
Hill was a remarkable creative administrator and one of the great public
servants of the century. He might not know a man from a bull's foot, but
he did know how to shape the world's postal service. A fortnight before
Hill's formal departure (he had actually been absent, his health failing,
for some months past), Trollope managed to write a letter to tell him so.[3]

It was a very handsome letter. The thought occurs, though it may be over-suspicious, was Trollope, just for once, being disingenuous or diplomatic?

He had a sturdy, honourable detestation of intrigue, flattery, or what he called toadying. In his literary career he did none of it, less than any of his contemporaries. But he was familiar with the official world from the inside. He couldn't avoid realizing that the succession in the top places at the Post Office was about to be decided. That was important for his friend John Tilley and for himself. Hill would have his say, possibly a predominant say. Whether Trollope also reflected that Hill would be about as likely to be mollified by a generous letter as by a copy of the Lusiad in Portuguese, is unguessable, but realistic men have their moments of illusion.

But anyway, the top appointment was made promptly, the day after Hill's departure.[4] This was the filling of Rowland Hill's own place. Government service procedure in the sixties is still not completely understood. In our times, while the Post Office remained a ministerial department, the Treasury would have been involved in this appointment. In Trollope's time, it may have been settled internally. Seniority – in which Trollope himself vehemently believed – counted for more than it would today. John Tilley, who had been Under (or Assistant) Secretary for some years, Hill's number two, duly got the job. This was entirely sensible, and must have been anticipated for over a year. Though Tilley, some time before, had been obliged to defend himself officially against criticism for Hill, he had been made Acting Secretary during Hill's illness. Tilley was a good civil servant, lucid, competent, sardonically humorous, distinctly literate in the Victorian manner, and incidentally one of Trollope's most loyal friends who had occasionally acted for him as a kind of amateur literary agent.

That left the number two position open. In his account of the proceedings, the wound still rankling, Trollope says that he applied for it. That is odd, by twentieth-century standards, when it would be taken for granted that any senior official would be considered as a matter of course. Presumably others applied. Once again, there seems to have been no hesitation. Tilley's appointment had been decided on 15 March, this one on 17 March.[5] The appointment went to Frank Ives Scudamore, the Post Office Librarian. Frederick Hill, like his brother, had been long absent on sick leave,[6] and was not considered.

Trollope considered this decision, and went on considering it, as a monstrous injustice. Scudamore was junior to himself, which to Trollope made the choice an insult. He, Trollope, had given the 'best years of his life' to the office. He had spent more of his energies on his Post Office duties than he had ever done on his second, literary, career. He certainly

[131]

believed that. It was, in a kind of external sense, true. He still had large and practical ideas for the extension of the postal services. Now he had been passed over, and he would never be able to carry them out.

There is no record that he asked Tilley, who must have known precisely what had happened, and who was at least in part responsible, for an explanation. Conceivably, it wasn't such an injustice after all. It is fairly easy to imagine sober cool-headed civil servants – of which Tilley himself was a nice specimen – talking competently about the problem. This is a difficult one, they might have said. On the one hand, no one doubted Trollope's conscientiousness. He had never neglected an official duty in his life. What he was paid for in the public service, he did, and more than that. He would have been outraged to think (as some gossips, including Yates, suggested) that he could have done otherwise. His colleagues knew it. They had spent many years with him. They could allow for his nuisance value at meetings, and Tilley above all had known him as the kindest and most sensitive of friends. When, nearly three years later, he left the Post Office they put it on the official record. He had been one of the most valuable of public servants, so the formal letter said, and nothing had been allowed to come in the way of his duty.

On the other hand, he had lived an eccentric life, even by the standards of the Victorian Civil Service. He was by now (1864) one of the three most celebrated novelists in England. The Post Office had given him an amiably free hand. He had hunted two or three days a week each winter, and somehow managed to fit in all his official work. Not even Sir Henry Taylor had done that: but then Trollope hadn't written *Philip van Artevelde*.

As number two, he would have been ready to renounce his hunting, and adjust himself, as he had once done, to ordinary office hours. But he had become a figure in London social life. Men like Tilley may reasonably have wondered whether he could give full attention to headquarters duties, which must have had their fair share of gritty routine. He would work out of conscience and duty, and he had his abundance of energy; but could he give the best of his mind? Alternatively, was Trollope, not totally immersed in the job, more useful than someone, not so interesting, who was?

That is how latter-day civil servants would have argued: and it is long odds that they would have reached the same conclusion. As a matter of fact, Scudamore was a distinctly able man, and an unusual one. Trollope is totally unfair to him in the autobiography. By a singular irony, Scudamore did resign from the Post Office in a huff ten years later.[7]

As soon as he heard the news, Trollope didn't regard the situation with detachment. He was deeply hurt, and very angry. He went immediately into action. He didn't show the beautiful tolerant judgment

The 'Larder' at the Returned Letter Office. Edmund Yates (inset right), *a younger and distinctly envious colleague of Trollope's, was responsible for this office*

with which, at precisely the same time, he was writing *The Last Chronicle of Barset*. Instead, he performed much more like a modern militant trade unionist. He gathered together his fellow Surveyors, and they concocted a Memorial demanding an increase in pay – their chief argument being that they spent extra time on 'special duties'. This Memorial was despatched on 8 April.[8] It was discussed at an official meeting of the Postmaster General on 18 April.[9] The Surveyors received a cool reply from Tilley, signed on 21 April,[10] turning down their application, and reminding them that other officials of the Post Office, not only Surveyors, were required to undertake special duties without additional pay.

Trollope was enraged. There is no doubt that he thought it was Tilley who had kept him out of the job. In a novel, he would have delicately examined Tilley's situation, having to decide on the fate of his oldest friend. In life, Trollope didn't feel like any such delicate examination. He brooded and seethed. On 8 July[11] he sent a 'remonstrance' to Lord Stanley, the Postmaster General, which in Civil Service practice had first to be considered by Tilley himself.

The 'remonstrance' takes a high place among foolish gestures made

[133]

by sensible and responsible men. It is about four thousand words long, furiously, badly, repetitively, written. 'I wish to remonstrate . . . I have a right to remonstrate . . .' It consists largely of an attack on Tilley in person. In his long experience of the Post Office, Trollope wrote, he had never seen an official document so studiously offensive in manner. Trollope remarked that he had known three other Secretaries, Sir Francis Freeling, Colonel Maberley, Sir Rowland Hill. None of them would have been capable of such an outrageous reply. When one remembers that Maberley and Hill had been Trollope's implacable enemies, that was not a conciliatory statement.

Trollope proceeded to the arguments about special duties. What special duties had officials at Headquarters ever executed? Trollope was punctilious enough to exempt his successful rival, Scudamore – 'always excepting Mr Scudamore,' says the 'remonstrance'. But what special duties had Mr Tilley himself executed? No doubt he had carried out his ordinary duties conscientiously and competently: but what special ones could he possibly claim? Trollope demanded that Mr Tilley should speak for himself and give an explicit answer.

Tilley wouldn't have been human if he hadn't been angry. He took the correct Civil Service step, and sent the 'remonstrance' to the Postmaster General, with a covering note, on 9 July,[12] allowing himself to describe the 'remonstrance' as 'this most intemperate letter from Mr Trollope'. Another official meeting, 11 July.[13] Again, they wouldn't have been human if they hadn't taken some comfort from a simple thought. This proved that, in selecting Scudamore, they had made the right choice. Behaviour like this really wouldn't have done.

Letter to Trollope 18 July,[14] drafted by Tilley. 'The Postmaster General observes with regret the tone of your appeal . . .'

Soon they all calmed down. Tilley thought of a way to pacify Trollope. Any suggestion of another trip abroad would tell him that he was still well-thought-of. There is a letter of Tilley's to the Postmaster General, 10 February 1865 (like a lot of Tilley's official letters, considerate and quietly amused: he was an exceptionally humane Civil Servant, ready to make allowances for all human frailties except drunkenness in letter-carriers).

> My dear Lord, I wrote to Trollope to ask him whether, in the event of your deciding to send someone to the East and offering the job to him, he would be willing to go.
>
> I send his answer, the interpretation of which is that he would readily go, and that he would consider an offer coming from you as an order, which he had no discretion to disobey.[15]

That reply of Trollope's, presumably quite humble, has not been traced, and the mission to the East never happened. But they were at peace. Lord Stanley was very fond of Trollope, and Tilley must have wished to heal a breach in friendship. Trollope's anger dimmed down. He didn't take a decision about resigning for a long time. For him this was a major one, in emotional terms as well as practical. Once he became commercially successful as a writer, he had been speculating whether he ought to leave the Post Office.

He loved the place. That isn't an overstatement. He was one of those men to whom institutions are the plinths of society, and who feel unprotected when they are no longer inside their own. Compare his relation – excessive to the minds of harder and more nomadic souls – with the Garrick Club. St Martin's-le-Grand hadn't been good to him: yet he felt at home when he climbed up to the senior official floor.

The old intimacy between Tilley and Trollope was as strong as ever as they passed into their sixties. By a pleasing trick of fate, Tilley asked Trollope's advice as to whether he should resign the Secretaryship when he got past retiring age. Trollope, with the utmost frankness, said No.[16] It would have been much more congenial working under Tilley, even without being his deputy, than it could have been under Rowland Hill. If Trollope had stuck out his final ten years, he would have been respected, uncriticized, indulged. But he didn't. He spent the best part of three years coming to a decision, and then went.

There were some practical arguments for doing so. From books, his earning power was at its peak. He had accumulated a certain amount of capital, something over twenty thousand pounds. He had been offered the editorship of a new magazine, which would bring in a thousand a year and which he couldn't take on if he remained in the Post Office. He would be free at last, and could earn more from miscellaneous writing.

Trollope, though, was a prudent and apprehensive man. If he resigned, it meant giving up his pension. To collect that, he had to stay till he was sixty (i.e. the summer of 1875). He would then receive something over a thousand per annum for life. This, together with the income on his capital, would provide against all vicissitudes (the value of money, we have to remember, was pretty constant all through the nineteenth century).

For a long time he was torn. Maybe the decision, like a good many others, was made before he realized it. In October 1867 he sent in his letter of resignation.[17] He says it was a day 'which to me was most melancholy'. Tilley, writing officially for the Postmaster General, replied in the stately and generous terms already referred to. The Post Office also made a polite gesture, presumably initiated by Tilley. Although Trollope was no longer an official, they asked him in the following year to conduct high-level negotiations with the American Postmaster General. In later days they would have secured him a decoration, but in the nineteenth century the Civil Service hadn't managed to expand the honours list. The Secretary of the Post Office got a knighthood, there was occasionally the odd C.B. but no one in the office as a rule got anything.[18]

At the precise time that he resigned (to be exact, two days earlier), he stepped into the editorship of the new *St Paul's Magazine*. That was a false move. He had none of Dickens' gifts as brilliant journalist-cum-impresario. Further, he didn't have a brilliant impresario publisher behind him, as George Smith had been with the *Cornhill*. Trollope's magazine was flat from the beginning, steadily lost money, and did him no good. He gave up the editorship within three years.

As soon as he was out of the official life, he made another false move. He stood for parliament, insisting that to enter the House of Commons had always been his greatest ambition and was, or should be, the greatest ambition of every genuine Englishman. Dickens simply couldn't understand him. The two of them were on slightly warmer terms as they grew older. They never really liked each other or each other's books, but they did reciprocal minor good turns. For instance, Trollope helped preside over the dinner to celebrate Dickens' second visit – his fatal visit – to America.[19]

Dickens, writing to Tom Trollope about his brother's parliamentary candidature, felt that Anthony had gone out of his mind. In fact, it was a fiasco. Trollope made uninspired speeches. He didn't get in and spent a lot of money. He was vexed, knowing that his judgment had gone askew, and beginning to worry, only a little, but just perceptibly, about money.

He might have been less fretted, in the coming years, if he had stayed at the Post Office. He would have written just as many books, for nothing could stop that. He wouldn't have had to forage round for commissions on travel books. Maybe he needed the security of old habits. To speak of the decline in the last dozen years of Trollope's life is to be over-dramatic, but there were times when he thought like that himself.

Opposite *The Village Post Office* (detail), *by Thomas Water-man Wood, 1873. Trollope visited such post offices on his trips to America. He was not unduly impressed by the American postal service.* Overleaf *Too Early, by James Tissot, 1870s*

16

FATHER AND SONS

When Trollope decided to relinquish Waltham, his lucky house, there were objective reasons for economy. His realistic common sense got allied to his natural tendency to foreboding, and that was a powerful combination. His editorship had failed, and he had lost that salary. He had, by his own choice, thrown away his Post Office salary and the prospect of a pension. He had wasted two thousand pounds by his appearance as Liberal candidate for Beverley. *Phineas Finn* and *He Knew He Was Right*, for which he had received hefty prices, hadn't earned anything like what he had been paid.

For the first time since before *The Warden* and *Barchester Towers*, he had lost money for a publisher. He knew the publishing business from the inside, and he suspected that soon he might not be able to demand his present prices. Which was true, though the fall-off wasn't steep, and he sold his books for considerable sums until the end.

He had been living handsomely at Waltham, not quite as handsomely as Dickens at Gadshill, but lavishly enough. There had been another major expense. Both his sons had recently cost large sums of money. We don't know as much as we should of Trollope as a father, but it would be absurd to doubt that he was an affectionate one, probably closer and more concerned than was usual among mid-Victorians. He asked G.H. Lewes' advice about sending them to school in Germany,[1] apparently not willing to put them through the same suffering he had known (a most un-Victorian attitude, except among eccentric aristocrats). He wrote intimate letters to the elder son Henry, and turned to him for support as old age seeped on.

The trouble was, neither of the boys seem to have had much of his ability, and Henry none of his tough will. Henry read for the Bar, was

Opposite *Kangaroo Hunt, Mount Zero, The Grampians, Victoria, by Edward Roper, 1880. In Queensland and New South Wales Trollope was taken out kangaroo hunting*

called, but didn't much fancy his chances. Possibly at Trollope's instigation, he then thought of publishing. He was bought a partnership in Chapman & Hall, and did some reading and editing there, rather like a contemporary American editor. That cost Trollope ten thousand pounds. After three or four years, Henry felt he didn't like publishing much either. So he got out, fortunately and rather surprisingly bringing most of the investment with him. For the rest of his life, which was a long one, he lived on the modest Trollope trust and as a modest man of letters.

Trollope kept trying to encourage him into more substantial bits of writing. He seems to have been a nice and lovable man. The oral tradition about him, still current in London in the thirties, was all in his favour. He had a reputation for extreme good nature. Sadleir dedicated his Trollope *Commentary* to Henry's memory.[2]

Frederick, the younger son, was a good deal more independent and self-willed. He wasn't academically bright, resented being outshone at school, and insisted, at the age of sixteen, on going out on his own to Australia. Australia had a singular attraction for the sons and relatives of eminent mid-Victorian writers, Dickenses, Arnolds, Kingsleys, Trollopes. There Fred became a sheep-farmer. This cost Trollope a good many more thousands of pounds. Fred worked indomitably, but made no money.

Trollope says that he was proud of his spirit and character.[3] That investment was all lost. Fred founded a large family, and his descendants are still living in Australia. By a complicated set of chances, the Trollope baronetcy descended to the son of Fred's third son, and remains in the family today.[4]

Even a man less far-sighted than Trollope would have had qualms after all the accumulating misfortunes. His judgment, once so good, had been erratic. The warnings were there. The luck was turning.

Like other active people, he found comfort in clear-cut decisions. Waltham must be given up. 'Would not a house in London be cheaper? There could be no doubt that my income would decrease and was decreasing . . . The thing was done and orders were given for the letting or sale of the house [Waltham]'.[5]

As it turned out, it took two years to sell Waltham, and Trollope lost another eight hundred pounds on the transaction. Things weren't going right. Meanwhile the house stood empty, and Trollope and Rose embarked, with stoical cheerfulness, for an eighteen-month trip to Australia.

Worries, major and minor, hadn't inhibited Trollope's work. He left the manuscript of *The Eustace Diamonds* (which proved to be one of his big successes) with *The Fortnightly*, and *Phineas Redux* and *An Eye For An Eye* with his son Henry, all to be published at suitable intervals. It

[138]

pleased Trollope to have provided this extra insurance for his family. On the voyage out, he wrote another novel, *Lady Anna.* As a matter of course, he had negotiated a contract for a travel book on Australia. He prepared this in his usual thorough and unskimping fashion, travelling all over the continent as few Englishmen had done.

He made an excellent book out of it, one of his best non-fiction works, highly regarded as soon as it came out. It had meant hard travel on a scale which most men of his age wouldn't have enjoyed, but Trollope was still an exceptionally robust and active man. We also get the feeling that arduous travel, like obsessive work, sometimes acted as a solvent for melancholy.

As for Rose, nothing in her previous life had trained her for existence

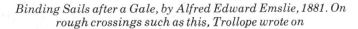

Binding Sails after a Gale, by Alfred Edward Emslie, 1881. On rough crossings such as this, Trollope wrote on

A Victorian selector's homestead in Australia. Fred's establishment, at the time of his parents' visit, would not have been markedly more comfortable

in the Australian bush, and she was a fastidious woman of nearly fifty. In her cool fashion, though, she was as tough and adaptable as her husband. They stayed six weeks on Fred's sheep farm. Living was, not surprisingly, rough and ready. The basic, in fact almost the only, food was mutton, washed down by lashings of tea. Victorians were used to mutton, which they consumed with a regularity unknown to us (you can find the traces all over Victorian fiction, old Warden Harding as well as young David Copperfield automatically dining off a mutton chop and *half a pint* of sherry, the Duke of Omnium (Plantagenet's uncle) eating only mutton at his own grand dinner, people all over the books hospitably invited to a meal of mutton). Still, for Rose Trollope, enough was enough. She couldn't abolish the mutton, but she did arrange for soup and salad, esoteric additions to the menu. While Fred, doing his best for his father, managed to substitute Australian wine for tea as his dinner drink.

In private, even Trollope admitted that he got tired of mutton. Though the evidence is scanty, we are left with the pleasant impression that

THE GOOD ST. ANTHONY
KEPT HIS EYES FIRMLY FIXED UPON HIS BOOK.
THE WAY THAT VERY FAST WRITER, MR. TROLLOPE, COLLECTED THE INFORMATION THAT
ENABLED HIM TO BRAND OUR GIRLS AS GONERILS AND REGANS.

Left *Cartoon from the Melbourne* Punch. *The Australian press believed that Trollope had libelled Australian women. Very strange, if they read* John Caldigate. Right *39 Montague Square*

Trollope had a real, perhaps a groping, affection for Fred. It may have been the kind of affection that parents sometimes have for not very clever, well-intentioned Benjamins. Certainly Trollope paid another visit to Australia three years later, and produced still more money, which was becoming still more of an effort, to help Fred in his struggle.

About Fred's attitude to his father, there is only the most vestigial of evidence. Yet the tone of Trollope's references is so benign and paternally happy that most of us would guess that Fred returned the affection and that the two of them were oddly, perhaps not articulately, easy together. One would have given something for a few of their letters to each other. So far as is known none exists.[6]

All in all, the Australian sojourn was a success. It refreshed Trollope's fund of interest and produced one of his better second-rank novels, *John Caldigate.*

When the Trollopes returned to England, at the end of 1872, they set about buying a house in Montague Square. Montague Square wasn't an

[141]

aristocratic quarter like Berkeley Square, Belgrave Square, Eaton Square. It was comfortable upper middle class, a place suitable for old Jolyon Forsyte. Trollope had lived like a modest country gentleman at Waltham: now, economizing, he was living like a modestly successful professional man. He liked the house. In his autobiography, written three years after he had moved in, he says that he hopes to spend the rest of his time there, and to die there.[7]

He would recognize Montague Square if he saw it today. It hasn't changed too much. It lies on the north side of Oxford Street and is a piece of very early nineteenth-century development, about 1815, later than most of Mayfair, a year or so later than its neighbour Bryanston Square, but earlier than Belgravia. It has the curious faintly wistful London bourgeois charm, and from number 39, Trollope's house,[8] one could look out over the long residents' garden and see the peeling plane trees.

He settled down into a characteristic pattern of living. He did not get up quite so early, but he still worked on his books before breakfast – from eight or thereabouts to nearly eleven. Breakfast was taken afterwards. One has to say 'worked on his books' because nowadays he didn't write them all by hand. He had an attentive, dutiful niece, Florence Bland, living in the house, and often he composed a novel by dictation, which she took down in longhand.

He had his quota of writers' hypersensitivity, and tore up the pages if she ventured a mild criticism. But the two of them seem to have enjoyed themselves, composing away, the London murk (much thicker then than now) outside the study window.

It would be hard, purely on textual grounds, to determine which of those later books were dictated and which written in his former manner. As a rule, dictation (compare a similar transition in Henry James) stands out plain enough. Dictated sentences sprawl, wander, meander more – just as an impromptu speech does. Only rigid training makes utterances orally precise.

The Duke's Children (published near the end of this last period) is one of the most elegant verbally of all Trollope's novels. It is a nice problem whether it was written or dictated.

For three years after moving into Montague Square – until the time, early in 1876, when he completed the autobiography – he went on hunting. He kept four horses in London, no doubt in some local mews. There were over a million domestic servants in London at this period, and there must have been a similar number of horses, all ensconced in the proliferating but now inconspicuous mews.

He hunted three days a week in the season, and he had to travel to the meets by train. His cab arrived for him at seven in the morning, he arrived back home from the railway station in time for dinner at eight.

[142]

(Dinner hours for the upper classes had anyway moved markedly later.) He weighed sixteen stone by now. Although he had become half deaf, his eyesight, always defective, wasn't appreciably worse. He says ruefully: 'This [hunting] has been work for a young man and a rich man, but I have done it as an old man and a comparatively poor man.'[9]

He was on call for all kinds of committees, social functions, dinner parties. In the afternoon he rode one of the horses from Montague Square to the Garrick Club, which isn't much less than two miles by the main streets. It was a good sight, fellow members said, to see the 'fine-looking old gentleman', as Julian Hawthorne called him,[10] dismounting outside the club, white-whiskered, ruddy-faced.

We know, as probably young Hawthorne didn't, that entering the club, cheerful at the prospect of his daily whist, he was feeling a load of anxiety shrugged away. Note the 'old gentleman'. Note that Trollope talks of himself as an old man. At this time he was not yet sixty. It is true that, if we met him, we would think of him as much older. Just as if we met Dickens at the corresponding age (Dickens died in 1870, still only fifty-eight) we should think of him as definitely old.

Left *A Memorable Whist Party at the Athenaeum.* (Left to right) *Trollope, Abraham Hayward, Right Hon. W. E. Forster, Sir George Jessel. Not as convivial as whist at the Garrick, but comforting enough.* Right *Sir Henry James (Lord James of Hereford), Trollope's closest friend in high politics*

Trollope was not so ravaged as Dickens. He hadn't exhausted himself by histrionic lectures, he was pretty hale into his late fifties, when Dickens was near death. Nevertheless modern medicine would have taken a prognostic look at both of them and set about trying to prolong their lives.

Dickens must have been walking about with grossly high blood pressure, years before his last suicidal lecture tours. Of course, he was so ferociously wilful that he would have been difficult to deter: but modern doctors know more about hypertension, would have used knowledge to frighten him and employed drugs without side effects. Trollope, much less intractable, would have been an easy patient. He would have been obediently taking the anti-tensive drugs when people still thought he was the picture of middle-aged health. That should have avoided some of the physical trouble in his sixties, and might have given him five or ten more years.

Opposite *Fox Hunters Meeting, the Hertfordshire Hunt, by James Pollard. 'During the winters of 1873, 1874 and 1875, I had my horses back in Essex, and went on with my hunting, always trying to resolve that I would give it up.'* Autobiography

17

CONFESSION AT SIXTY

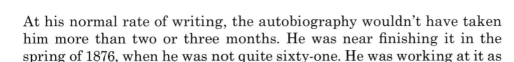

At his normal rate of writing, the autobiography wouldn't have taken him more than two or three months. He was near finishing it in the spring of 1876, when he was not quite sixty-one. He was working at it as a protection against the shadows closing in and also a kind of defiance, his own strange form of boasting.

The shadows were closing in. Many times the calm, rational, stoical statements don't hide the melancholy beneath. He had just decided to give up hunting. Trollope wasn't a hypochondriac (Dickens was the opposite of a hypochondriac, whatever that is), he had been unusually free from illness, but he may already have felt the premonitions of physical decay.

There were, however, closer shadows than that. His literary reputation – and just as much, perhaps more, his popular success – had been the solid basic satisfaction of his life. At moments now, not constantly, he felt that both were draining away.

There was some objective validity in this, but not as much as we are inclined to think. In one of the most interesting chapters in Sadleir's study,[1] he provides a professional opinion. Sadleir was an experienced publisher, and here, as on bibliographical topics, he speaks with considerable authority. In publishing circles, he is sure, Trollope was being quietly written off. He was no longer a great property. Yet publishing circles are fairly esoteric, and Sadleir, living in them, may have exaggerated their influence. The press, which he can't have had the opportunity to study in detail,[2] had, as has already been mentioned, turned much less sharply against Trollope than Sadleir thought.

The general tone, from *Barchester Towers* onwards, had always been affectionate, a kind of surprised admiration blending with a faint air of condescension. It didn't change overmuch until his death. For instance, *The Eustace Diamonds* (1873) was as well received in public as any of his novels, and the private press (i.e. the talk among literary people, always a good indication) was very warm. This was just as true, probably more true, of *The Duke's Children* (published in 1880, three years before his death), which received enthusiastic praise – to the credit of all concerned.

There were exceptions. *The Prime Minister* (1876) was dismissed with

ANTONIUS TROLLOPIUS.
AUTHOR OF THE LAST CHRONICLES OF CICERO.
"O Rare for Antony!"—SHAKSPEARE.

A cartoon from Punch

contempt. This hurt Trollope bitterly. It happened that he was finishing the autobiography at the time, and for the first, and only, time in his life he felt like taking the advice of one of his critics, which was to give up writing for good. That was a mood which didn't last, but the wound did. He wasn't as resilient as he used to be, and he couldn't understand it. It is still difficult to understand. *The Prime Minister* has its longueurs, and Emily Wharton is something of a trial, but it is an admirable book.

The political scenes are the best in the Palliser series, and the development of the Duke (Plantagenet Palliser) is one of Trollope's subtlest triumphs. Tolstoi, who must have read the book in English[3] soon after publication, thought, as we have seen, that it was one of the most remarkable of all novels. What a pity that Trollope didn't know (though, come to think of it, he was not likely to know much about Tolstoi, whose name was only just reaching the West).

[146]

Incidentally, Tolstoi's immersion in *The Prime Minister* sets a delicate and possibly insoluble problem in literary detection. At about the same time, though it can't be dated precisely to the exact month, as Tolstoi was reading *The Prime Minister*, he was himself getting towards the end of *Anna Karenina*. Did he write the description of Anna's suicide before or after he read about Lopez's? Tolstoi was as original and uninfluenceable as a writer can be, but an episode of that bizarre nature (exceptionally well done by Trollope) could have left its mark. Tolstoi might have considered that the English were likely to be expert about suicides on railway lines.

The Prime Minister apart, Trollope wasn't so badly treated by the critics, although he may have felt, and in his sensitive fine-nerved fashion probably did feel, that whispers of depreciation, as yet inaudible, would soon make themselves heard. *The Way We Live Now*, one of his

Opposition Bench, 1880. Only a few years from the Duke of Omnium's administration. When he was writing the Palliser novels Trollope said: 'I had humbly to crave [the speaker's] permission for a seat in the gallery, so that I might become conversant with the ways and doings of the House in which some of my scenes were to be placed.' Autobiography

most remarkable novels and in some ways the most unusual, received some fresh denunciations, some of them for non-literary reasons.

It is likely, however, that the falling off of his public depressed him more. Victorian novelists, including the greatest, were more in touch with their public than their successors have been. Public esteem meant more to them than their critical reputation: public esteem as an emotional link, a kind of love. This was true above all of Dickens, but Trollope felt it too, less outpouringly but deeply. Of the major figures, George Eliot may have been the most immune.

There were obvious reasons for this closeness between writer and readers. The reading public was much smaller than it shortly became. The writers lived among them, they were part of their society, the not very large, educated, predominantly prosperous society of the mid-century. The writers made concessions to it. Dickens, Trollope, Thackeray, couldn't have contemplated offending it by telling all they knew of the sexual life. It would have been psychologically impossible, as much so as telling blue stories in a drawing room – which, since they were working for just such an audience, it would have closely resembled.

Sometimes they were irked by these restraints. Trollope would have liked to be totally candid about Lucina Roanoke and Mabel Grex. But it is arguable that they gained more than they lost by this rapport and interaction. A writer was not a solitary voice talking into a vacuum.

So they were all sensitive, more than sensitive, to a decline in their public. Dickens, as confident of his genius as any writer has ever been, was nevertheless profoundly upset when *Martin Chuzzlewit* didn't sell, and promptly sent Martin to America. Trollope had nothing like Dickens's confidence. Decline in sales gnawed away at his self-esteem, never strong enough. And, of course, a decline in sales was at least a practical nuisance, and a warning for the future.

Actually, this decline, though real, wasn't anything like disastrous. His biggest payment per volume (remember these were outright sales, not advances on royalties) was two thousand eight hundred pounds for *The Claverings,* 1867, a two-volume novel. For three volumes he received in 1869 three thousand two hundred each for *Phineas Finn* and *He Knew He Was Right.* That can be taken as the height of his earning power. In 1876, the year of the autobiography, he obtained two thousand five hundred for *The Prime Minister,* and eighteen for *The American Senator* next year. Sadleir suggests that this was achieved only by hard bargaining, switching publishers, and being serialized in less prestigious maga-

Opposite *A Pleasant Corner, by John Callcott Horsley, 1864.*
*A spirited girl, like Ayala, wished that women were not
secluded – the quiet protest gathering strength*

[148]

zines. In 1879 he could still contract for eighteen hundred pounds for *John Caldigate*. For shorter novels, right at the end of his life he had to squeeze out lesser sums.

For certain, the market was ebbing away from him, but not catastrophically. For certain also, in the final four or five years he was becoming increasingly obsessed about money. He wrote many letters to his son Henry about quite insignificant payments that they were receiving from investments. Yet, in his heartier and less anxious moments, he must have known that (*a*) money was not a genuine problem, and that, if he didn't write another word, he could continue living comfortably at his present level, (*b*) he could still sell his books and earn a fair literary income as long as he cared to write.

At other moments, those Philinthe-like reflections would have been no consolation. He was capable of taking all that was happening as symptoms of failure – the critical attacks (pretty vicious by nineteenth-century standards) on *The Way We Live Now* and above all on *The Prime Minister*, which was a work he cherished – the drop in his market value – a subliminal sense that he wasn't as healthy as he looked. Melancholy could be laughed away in company, perhaps less often with his wife. Sometimes it shattered the stoical appearance. There is a passage in the autobiography which, a hundred years later, is still painful to read.

> Since that time [his arrival in Ireland] who has had a happier life than mine? Looking round upon all those I know, I cannot put my hand upon one. But all is not over yet, and mindful of that, remembering how great is the agony of adversity, how crushing the despondency of degradation, how susceptible I am myself to the misery coming from contempt, – remembering also how quickly good things may go and evil things come – I am often again tempted to hope, almost to pray that the end may be near.[4]

When he wrote that he was sixty. It is hard to think of anything quite like it. We must, of course, remember that he didn't live continually in such a mood. We misunderstand high-spirited robust depressives if we forget the fluidity of his kind of temperament, the surges, fluctuations, outbursts, flares of cheerfulness and selfless interest. He could very well have written that and gone off to be the boisterous life and soul of the Garrick whist table.

His cheerfulness with others (cheerfulness rather than happiness) and flow of interest never seem to have left him. Nevertheless, that sombre mood, though not continuous, was part of his existence. His greatest novels wouldn't have had their depths without it. On the other hand, it didn't make it easier for him to strengthen himself against decline.

Travel, Australia again, South Africa, Iceland, hard work – those were his good old prescriptions against the dark. Hunting had gone but

Left *Sir John Tilley, at the age when he was writing to Trollope, asking advice as to whether to resign the Secretaryship of the Post Office. The appearance of age is deceptive: Tilley was in robust health.* Right *Trollope*

nothing else. His creative energy hadn't damped down. He was writing as productively as ever. And what is important to remember, as enthusiastically. There is a letter – already briefly mentioned – dated April 1878 to John Tilley, more self-revelatory, less tight-lipped and misleadingly hard-baked than anything he had previously allowed himself to say about his vocation.

Trollope was sixty-three, Tilley nearly sixty-five. Tilley, the impeccable civil servant, had rather surprisingly written to say that he was thinking of giving up the Chief Secretaryship at the Post Office. He could stay another two years, and then retire on full pay. But he was getting old. He wanted the judgment of his oldest friend. Trollope replied by return, at his firmest and most affectionate. After saying (probably with some inner feeling) that Tilley seems to have the health of a man of forty, Trollope goes on: 'If the work goes against the grain with you, that may be reason for leaving it. But if it be easy with you I do not think the mere fact of your age should induce you to leave it; nor the fact that your pay would come to you though the work were abandoned.

'*You say of me; that I would not choose to write novels unless I were paid. Most certainly I would; much rather than not write them at all.*'

Trollope continues that the only considerations are Tilley's happiness and his duty. Trollope reminds him, gently but intimately, that he has no

[151]

other interests. He won't be happy if he has nothing but books to turn to. Trollope, also gently, says that money 'should not count as anything. The Post Office has been so beneficent to you that you owe it everything.

It is to Tilley's credit that he took the advice. It would have been a support to Trollope if he himself had had a sensible friend to whom he was prepared to listen. He still had the joy of writing, but most of the pleasures were fading out as his health got worse. About this time his health was deteriorating too perceptibly for him to brush off the signs, much less for his wife.

The doctors called it asthma. No doubt it was a cardiac condition. Then another doctor diagnosed angina, and a specialist contradicted him. Rose Trollope was frightened, but though he was brave in illness as Dickens was, if rather more tractable, he wasn't easy to manage. A friend, ready to be as tough with him as he was with Tilley, would have tried to manage his affairs so as to leave him with some of the emollients of old age. He didn't want to dine out often now, but he would have been cheered up by agreeable company.

That didn't happen. Victorian doctors were moderately homicidal. It still seems surprising that they were so bad at diagnosing the heart and artery complaints of aging men. They must have seen enough of them. At that time, of course, they couldn't have done much to cope with them. As their one resource, they were abnormally confident about the therapeutic value of a minor change in climate.

Think of the meaningless journeys that Victorian sufferers were exposed to – like Trollope's sister Cecilia, Tilley's first wife, despatched to Genoa, Florence, bustled half dead to Rome, before she came home to die. Trollope's doctor said that Hampshire was the place to cure his asthma. He and Rose may have felt that it would be another economy to give up the house in Montague Square. In any case they obeyed the doctors and in 1880 bought a reconstructed farmhouse in the remote countryside, near Petersfield. It was to be their last move.

18

TROLLOPE'S ART: II

I

Trollope's major gift was his percipience, and his art depended upon it, to an extent perhaps unique among novelists. He had, of course, to find means, technical means, to use it when he wanted, first to depict, then to explain and interpret his characters – or rather the human beings whom, in his imagination, he held so unremittingly in mind.

As he said himself, he knew that that kind of human concentration was his special talent.[1] Since his confidence wasn't invulnerable enough, he made boss shots in other forms which required quite different gifts – like the folly of *Brown, Jones and Robinson*, or, very near the end of his life, an absurd attempt at futurist fiction, *The Fixed Period*. But really he knew, and once said clearly, as we have seen, that any merit he had lived in his great characters.

He had acute self-knowledge – otherwise he couldn't have known others as he did – and there he was, as usual, judging himself right. Other novelists have had unusual percipience, though it hasn't come to many with so little strain, so much as a natural grace.[2] It would be ridiculous to suggest that Tolstoi, Dostoevsky, Proust didn't include percipience among their range of gifts. Also Stendhal, Galdós, Jane Austen – with more effort, Henry James and George Eliot – some others, though not so many as one might think. With all of those just mentioned, however, it wasn't a dominant, much less a solitary, gift. We should still read Tolstoi for the astonishing power of his senses and his Jehovianic vision of life, if he were only normally sensible about his characters. Also Proust, for his brilliant intelligence and his recall of the physical world: Dostoevsky for the depth and swirl of his psychological imagination (different from percipience, which he also possessed). And so on.

None of that applies to Trollope. As has been stated simply in chapter thirteen, if his primary gift is stripped away or isn't recognized (as it often hasn't been) there isn't much left. He would be just a readable, informative nineteenth-century novelist, nothing more. He is much more.

It rests precisely on how highly one values his sense of individual human beings, where one ranks him as a novelist. If you value it highly, as one of the supreme requirements of a novelist, then you rank him very high. It is customary for orthodox persons to say that they would never consider making ranking orders of writers: and then, in the next breath, by implication they do just that.

When the present writer is playing that game, he invents a special category for Trollope, a little beneath, and aside from, the very greatest. But in the aspect where he and Tolstoi were trying to do identical things, it is interesting to compare him with the greatest of all.

To anyone starting fresh on Trollope, there is a fairly easy test of whether the above estimate can be justified. There are forty-seven novels, which is too many. It is obviously elementary sense to read one or two carefully, and more than once. Trollope, like all writers plain and lucid on the surface, deep beneath, needs reading for different interpretations and values. Though it isn't conventional advice, the best lead-in is probably with one of the less exacting novels, say *The Duke's Children* or *Framley Parsonage*. There you will find him at his most externally sharp and least disturbing. Then *Barchester Towers* or *Orley Farm*. Then *The Last Chronicle of Barset*.

If at that point you cannot see anything in Trollope, give it up. He is not for you. You are not in tune. You may have all the other virtues known to man, moral and aesthetic, but you can't share his percipience. Possibly you think that, once you have grown up, you have shorthand answers about human beings. Well, some great writers have thought that. In many, they arouse passionate response. To others, they lack the tentative, exploratory sense which gets nearer to the truth. That Trollope had.

Externally, his technical means began in the same fashion as those of all novelists who have had an intention similar to his. He was a good observer. This has to be qualified. Very few novelists have had the total visual recall of, say, Simenon. Trollope doesn't seem to have picked up much in art galleries, though he tried hard. His eye for architecture was as dull as Jane Austen's. But he was a good observer of his people. When he was interested, his eyes and ears (most of all ears) were acute.

He knew by instinct, as all realistic writers have always known, that the bodies of human beings aren't to be separated from their souls. Trollope's descriptions of men and women in the flesh, not elaborate but scrupulous, are part of total comprehension. There is no single case, in all his vast cast of characters, where someone so described couldn't have had the personality, mind, spirit, which Trollope is proceeding to examine. That is often not at all true in the work of novelists less intuitive

*Defendant and Counsel, by W. F. Yeames, 1895. Possibly
Madame Goessler consulting Phineas Finn's lawyers*

or less experienced. It is absolutely true in Tolstoi and Proust, and nearly
always in Balzac.

Trollope saw his people clearly and carefully: but his great resource –
his greatest technical resource in projecting characters – was his ear.
That is, his ability to suggest in his dialogue the tone of spoken speech,
and of each different person's spoken speech. This is perhaps the most
useful piece of technical equipment a novelist can possess, and it is more
than technical. A novelist doesn't get so absorbed in others' speech unless he is listening obsessively. Incidentally, what he finally represents
as dialogue on paper bears only a vestigial resemblance to a tape recording. An actual conversation, as recorded on tape, would be intolerable if
written down. That kind of naturalism has been tried and has disastrously failed, except in the smallest doses.

Curiously enough, the halts and hums and lack of conclusion of real
live speech iron out the differences between personal tones of voice,
which is what a novelist needs above all. Realistic dialogue in novels is a

peculiarly subtle branch of art, and has to sound right to the ear while being guided by a concealed convention.

Trollope was one of the masters of such dialogue. When Henry James said that Trollope had a good ear, he was using that as a metaphor for Trollope's general sensitivity: but James, who was skilful at dialogue himself, recognized the art of Trollope's. Dickens also wrote some splendid dialogue, but, as usual between him and Trollope, there is a revealing contrast. They listened to others in different fashions. Dickens listened like a mimic with brilliant concentration and, like a mimic, picked the parts of a speech idiom which amused and fascinated him most. Again like a mimic, he was tempted to reiterate his effects or over-stress a single effect. Whereas Trollope just listened with acceptance.

The art of dialogue can, of course, be studied profitably only in textual detail. This isn't the place for it, and there is an overwhelming amount of dialogue in both Dickens and Trollope, especially Trollope. A thesis on the dialogue of Victorian masters (those two, George Eliot, Henry James, would be quite enough, with perhaps a side glance at a good writer whose dialogue was bad, such as Charlotte Brontë or Collins) could be valuable. It would deal with the resemblances and differences between educated speech of the mid-nineteenth century with that of our own – and could scarcely help showing, as has been mentioned already, that the resemblances are far greater than the differences.

A good preliminary, likely to emphasize this point, is to listen to someone reading Trollope or Dickens aloud. Dickens sounds far more natural, and in many passages more nearly contemporary in tone, than one would have thought. Trollope sounds entirely natural, and it is a jolt when, quite rarely, there is a phrase we shouldn't use.

Perhaps there is room here for a couple of fairly brief passages of Trollopian dialogue. They give some idea of the scope for textual analysis. They come from *Doctor Thorne*, Trollope's first major success though not one of his better books, and are chosen to show exchanges between the same two characters.

One is Mr Gresham, 'the first commoner in Barsetshire', a member of the untitled landed gentry, a group for whom Trollope had a particular fondness. He has run through a great deal of the family fortune. The other is Dr Thorne himself, a good but impoverished doctor, himself a relative of an old county family. Mr Gresham turns to him as adviser and confidant. The commentary has been deleted, and the dialogue printed as in a play. The italics represent expressions which we should not use at the present time. ('Did not' and so on are reproduced as in the nineteenth-century text. They were of course pronounced 'didn't' etc., exactly as we should.)

[156]

Mr Gresham: You did not see Humbleby as you came in?

Dr Thorne: No I did not; and if you *will* take my advice you will not see him now; at any rate with reference to the money.

Mr Gresham: I tell you I must get it from someone; you say Scatcherd won't let me have it.

Dr Thorne: No, Mr Gresham; I did not say that.

' "*I must have ten or twelve thousand pounds; ten at the very least,*" *said the squire.' Illustration from* Dr Thorne

Mr Gresham: Well, you said what was as bad. Augusta is to be married in September, and the money must be had. I have agreed to give Moffatt six thousand pounds and he is to have the money down in hard cash.

Dr Thorne: Six thousand pounds. Well, I suppose that isn't more than your daughter should have. But then, five times six are thirty: thirty thousand pounds will be a large sum to make up. [There were five Gresham daughters.]

Mr Gresham: That Moffatt is a *griping, hungry fellow.* I suppose Augusta likes him, and, as regards money, it is a good match.

[157]

Dr Thorne: If Miss Gresham loves him that is everything. I am not in love with him myself: but then, I am not a young lady.

Mr Gresham: The de Courcys are very fond of him. Lady de Courcy says that he is a perfect gentleman, and thought *very much of* in London.

Dr Thorne (with quiet sarcasm, lost on Mr Gresham): Oh! if Lady de Courcy says that, of course it's all right.

With minor verbal emendations, that little scene could go on the London stage tomorrow. The financial arrangements would seem strange, but the dialogue could have been written in 1975.

Some weeks later, Mr Gresham had still not raised the money.

Mr Gresham: You wouldn't have me allow my daughter to lose this match for the sake of a few thousand pounds? It will be *well* at any rate to have one of them settled. Look at that letter from Moffatt (gives letter, which says Moffatt can't and won't marry without the money, to Dr Thorne). It may be all right, but in my time gentlemen *were not used* to write such letters as that to each other.

(Dr Thorne shrugs his shoulders.)

Mr Gresham (continuing): I told him that he should have the money: and one would have thought that would have been enough for him. Well: I suppose Augusta likes him. I suppose she *wishes* the match; otherwise I would give him such an answer to that letter as *should* startle him a little.

Dr Thorne: What settlement is he to make?

Mr Gresham: Oh, that's satisfactory enough; couldn't be more so; a thousand a year and the house at Wimbledon for her; that's all very *well*. But such a lie, you know, Thorne. He's rolling in money, and yet he talks of his *beggarly* sum as though he couldn't possibly stir without it.

Dr Thorne: If I might venture to speak my mind –

Mr Gresham: Well?

Dr Thorne: I should be inclined to say that Mr Moffat wants to cry off himself.

Mr Gresham: Oh, impossible, quite impossible. In the first place, he was so very anxious for the match. In the next place, it is such a *great thing* for him. And then, he would never dare; you see, he *is dependent* on the de Courcys for his seat.

Dr Thorne: But suppose he loses his seat?

Mr Gresham: But there is not much fear of that, I think. Scatcherd may be a very fine fellow, but I think they will hardly return him at Barchester.

Dr Thorne: I don't understand much about it, but such things do happen.

[158]

Mr Gresham: And you believe that this man *absolutely* wants to *get off the match*; *absolutely* thinks of playing such a trick as that on my daughter – on me?

Those passages were written well over a hundred years ago. It continues to be surprising that the spoken language of educated Englishmen should have changed so little. Points to notice, in preparatory to a fine-structure study of Victorian dialogue – (*i*) the number of idioms (e.g. hard cash, rolling in money) which have come down quite unchanged, (*ii*) words which have been replaced, e.g. 'absolutely' where we should say 'actually',[3] (*iii*) the loosening of our syntax. Victorians certainly wrote, and on the evidence of Trollope (and Dickens) used in speech, more subjunctives than we do; and they appear to have used correct futures and conditionals where we make do with the present tense (or sometimes, strangely, with the past). Compare Dr Thorne's 'If you will take my advice' to 1975 English – 'If you take my advice'. Syntax remaining in colloquial, cultivated mid-nineteenth-century English seems to have been about the same as in modern French.

There was another point, not exemplified in these passages, which were selected more or less at random. A sprinkling of Trollopian expressions, now lost in English-English speech, have survived in educated American-English. Trollope's aristocrats say 'gotten'. A more interesting case is the use of 'quite' – as in for example 'I was quite pleased to get your letter'. In Trollope, and in contemporary American, the 'quite' is to be read as 'very'. In English-English, *circa* 1975, it would sound remarkably cold: 'quite' has for some time taken on a depreciatory intonation. There are many similar examples. The manners of Trollope's privileged classes were much closer to their present-day American equivalents than their English ones. Archdeacon Grantly would say that 'Mrs Grantly and I look forward to seeing you'. An English archdeacon today would use her Christian name.

This disquisition, though interesting to the present writer, may not be so to anyone else, and had better be closed. The topic of novel dialogue, however, is well worth informed attention. The only real importance here is that Trollope had at his command a beautiful aid to projection (and representation) of character. This came partly through a deliberate and trained technique, but more through a kind of invisible grace, that is, his disinterested patient absorption in other people.

II

Which leads straight to the two main problems which Tolstoi had to face and all realistic novelists, major or minor, after him. Trollope had to face them too, but they didn't cost him any strain. One of them probably should have cost him more, but he walked through both propelled by the same invisible grace.

In order to translate his percipience into art, that is into fictional people whom we both see and understand, he knew as it were by instinct that external presentation was only the beginning. It was necessary but not sufficient. Speech could reveal something more, but not enough. Trollope, in this like all major novelists of character, was not a behaviourist. The human being wasn't expressed completely by what he said and did. How to get further?

The first problem is the approach which the novelist makes to each human being. To Trollope this was as natural as breathing. You had to be as direct as God would let you. Men, certainly not writers, weren't clever enough to be subtle: the human being you were looking at was complex enough without the writer adding to it. So you confronted him as straightforwardly as you confronted yourself. There could be no self-assertion or (which is a particular example of assertion) the assertion of style. The writer had to subdue himself. There must be nothing – as Lawrence said in a different context – between him and it. ('It' to Trollope would be the person he was trying to understand.)

That sounds easy. It was fairly easy, given Trollope's temperament. It wasn't at all easy for Tolstoi, which was one of the reasons he admired Trollope so much. Tolstoi had a monstrous ego which had to be subjugated, subjugated above all if he was going to accept and understand his own characters. In *War and Peace*, the megalomaniac ego has its fling, when Tolstoi gives Olympian instruction about the insignificance of Napoleon or the flux of history. But he conquers it when he is standing before his own fictional people, standing as humbly and unobtrusively as Trollope himself. That Tolstoi can do this is one of the magnificent triumphs of art. It wasn't an effort to Trollope, whose ego, as has been examined, was weak, often too much so for his own well-being. It was first nature to him to sit back, study, and absorb. He didn't have any desire to govern others' lives. Tolstoi did. Tolstoi was, however, a highly conscious artist. To depict and explore those others, one had, temporarily at least, to forget about governing them. In his two great novels, he committed himself to what Trollope could do so naturally.

As a conscious artist, Tolstoi saw some of the answer (not the whole of it) in terms of language. In his effortful fashion, he set to work to hammer out, for the revelation of character, the simplest possible style. 'Hammer out' seems a cliché, but it does describe many of his effects. Anyone who

Opposite A Summer's Day in Hyde Park (detail), by J. Ritchie, 1858. On such a day there, Lily Dale saw the man she loved

has examined the manuscripts of his novels will see how time and time again he deletes a picturesque word and repeats one already used. It was one of the most thorough, and in appearance sacrificial, revisions in literary history. Though it has struck some critics as monstrous, yet for his purpose, the purpose of ultimate directness, it was of course right. When he indulged himself, he was one of the most eloquent of writers and he was writing in a peculiarly eloquent language. In dealing with his characters he wasn't indulging himself. He was cutting out everything except telling the truth.

Trollope didn't need to make this effort. For exactly the same purpose his lucid and undecorated English (often under-rated and its flexibility quite missed) was perfectly adequate. So was Stendhal's business-like French. So, Spanish speakers tell us, was Galdós's language. It was a manner which, by nature or effort, many of the greatest students of character found for themselves.

The second problem was far more difficult. Here none of these masters was able to cope completely, and no one has been able to, down to the present day. How do you express what is passing through anyone's mind? Not only in critical circumstances, such as Archdeacon Grantly's at his father's bedside, but in any field of mental existence, when something is happening in a person's solitary mind. What is it like? Flow or to-and-fro commotion or discontinuous jumps? How much does its nature vary from person to person? It has sometimes been called the stream of consciousness, but that may be misleading. It is probably not always a stream, and only partly, in the strictest sense, conscious. It is certainly not always verbal, and for many people not often so. How much is it to be communicated in words? How much is that worth doing?

Since Stendhal, psychological novelists have given different answers to these questions. Probably none is totally satisfactory. It is quite likely that there isn't a single answer. Two of the greatest psychological novelists, Dostoevsky and Proust, chose methods which in effect side-stepped the problem, as though they didn't think it worth while to meet it head on. Dostoevsky let his people explain parts of their mental existence, as one might do in a wildly articulate extension of ordinary speech. No one ever spoke quite as Ivan Karamazov spoke to Alyosha in the garden, but from those great speeches one can infer the content – though not perhaps the structural nature – of Ivan's solitary thought. Proust used his own commentary, the play of his analytical mind, to do much the same. Neither of them tried to show directly the actual moment-by-moment events of

Opposite *The Proposal, by William Powell Frith, 1853. It was because of such demeanours of English girls that Kate Field came as a treat!*

mental experience (though Tolstoi did try once or twice, as with Prince Andrei lying wounded on the battlefield after Borodino).

For the present writer, the Dostoevsky and Proust methods carry more meaning than any attempts at direct representation, but this is a highly subjective matter and may very easily depend on the nature of one's own mental events. For a good many, it is certain that some direct representation either suggests the stuff of mental experience, or even immediately conveys it. The greatest of these head-on attempts was made by Joyce. Here is an example from the first part of *Ulysses*:

> Mr Bloom put his face forward to catch the words. English. Throw them the bone. I remember slightly. How long since your last Mass? Gloria and Immaculate Virgin. Joseph her spouse. Peter and Paul. More interesting if you understood what it was all about. Wonderful organization certainly, goes like clockwork. Confession. Everyone wants so. Then I will tell you all. Penance. Punish me, please. Great weapon in their hands. More than doctor or solicitor. Woman dying to. And I schschschschschsch and did you chachachachacha? And why did you? Look down at her ring to find an excuse. Whispering gallery walls have ears. Husband learned to his surprise. God's little joke. Then out she comes. Repentance skin deep. Lovely shame. Pray at an altar. Hail Mary and Holy Mary. Flowers, incense, candles melting. Hide her blushes. Salvation Army blatant imitation. Reformed prostitute will address the meeting. How I found the Lord. Square-headed chaps those must be in Rome: they work the whole show. And don't they rake in the money too? Bequests also: to the P.P. for the time being in his absolute discretion. Masses for the repose of my soul to be said publicly with open doors. Monasteries and convents.[4]

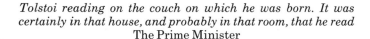

Tolstoi reading on the couch on which he was born. It was certainly in that house, and probably in that room, that he read The Prime Minister

The fundamental strategy is simple and uncircuitous. It takes the mental processes as atomic or discrete, with individual events happening in sequence, each in a present moment of time. Each event is then represented by a verbal correlative, in what scientists might call a one-to-one correspondence: or, as the Joyce mental experience is largely, not exclusively, oral, the event and the verbal correlative fuse, as one and the same thing. 'Woman dying to. And I schschschschschsch and did you chachachachacha?' Here Bloom's mental events and the words are pretty completely fused.

To many, – and in particular, perhaps, to many of high aesthetic sensibility – this is a totally satisfactory rendering of mental experience. For a good many others, it is not so. Theirs doesn't happen very much in that fashion, certainly not often and not as a continuous process: it is usually less discrete, less momentary, less verbal and less immediately expressible in verbal terms. It contains a far greater element of un-verbalized expectations.

It appears more and more likely that the nature of the process varies a great deal from person to person. At present we have nothing but intro-spective delving to go on, and by its nature that has its limitations. Using the introspective mind to report on the operations of the mind may be rather like standing in a bucket and pulling oneself up by the handle.

Writers have to do their best. To many sensibilities Joyce did the ultimate best (he was by no means the first to use that kind of one-to-one correspondence, but he did it with more mastery than his predecessors).[5] No one would claim that Trollope did the ultimate best in a different attack on the mental process: but he made his own beginning, and what this beginning led to can be seen when he came to examine the mind of Mr Crawley or Lady Mabel Grex.

Trollope didn't find an elaborate way round the problem, in the manner of Dostoevsky or Proust. His own mind was too direct for that, just as in his primary approach to human beings. Things went on in people's thoughts, and had to be communicated – so one must have a shot at it. But it would not have occurred to him, even if he had written at a later period in the novel's history, to attempt a record of moment-by-moment mental events. Not that he was naïve: few men less naïve have ever lived. He was interested, however, in other mental activities. If he had thought about it at all, he would have assumed that a study of the im-mediate present (even if his own immediate present was radically dif-ferent from Joyce's) would cut out all in which he was most interested. First, human personality as a whole. Next, some way after, the elements in mental processes which result in any moral choice or moral action.

So for his purpose he developed a form of psychological streaming. Take examples from an early novel, *The Small House at Allington*.

[163]

Adolphus Crosbie is a man of personality, some ability, and considerable lack of natural strength (Trollope knew a lot about infirmity of purpose). He has been staying in the Dale house, and Lily, the charming, witty, strong-willed, second daughter, has fallen deeply in love with him. He has fallen in love with her too, to the extent of asking her to marry him. They are engaged. She has no money. He is a rising civil servant, earning eight hundred pounds per annum (in the 1850s, a high salary for a young man) and is professionally and socially ambitious.

He goes to dinner with Squire Dale at the Great House.

Crosbie, when he went up to dress for dinner, fell into one of the melancholy fits of which I have spoken. Was he absolutely about to destroy all the good that he had done for himself throughout the past years of his hitherto successful life? Or rather as he had last put the question to himself more strongly, – was it not the case that he had already destroyed all that success? His marriage with Lily, whether it was to be for good or bad, was now a settled thing, and was not to be regarded as a matter admitting of any doubt. To do the man justice, I must declare that in all these moments of misery he still did the best he could to think of Lily herself as a great treasure which he had won, – as of a treasure which should, and perhaps would, compensate him for his misery. But there was the misery very plain. He must give up his clubs, and his fashion, and all that he had hitherto gained, be content to live a plain, humdrum, domestic life, with eight hundred a year, in a small house full of babies. It was not the kind of Elysium for which he had tutored himself. Lily was very nice, very nice indeed. She was, as he said to himself, 'by yards, the nicest girl that he had ever seen'. Whatever might now turn up, her happiness should now be his first care but as for his own, – he began to fear the compensation would hardly be perfect. 'It is my own doing' he said to himself, intending to be rather noble at the purport of his soliloquy, 'I have trained myself for other things, – very foolishly. Of course I must suffer, – suffer damnably, but she will never know it. Dear, sweet, innocent, pretty little thing!'[6]

He moves on from the Dales to Courcy Castle. The Courcys are among Trollope's most selfish aristocrats. They have a kind of style. They also have several unmarried daughters, the youngest, Alexandrina, in her late twenties, a year or so older than Crosbie. Crosbie enjoys himself in the first days there and brushes away, in conversation with one of the Courcy sons, but without quite denying them, the rumours that he has recently become engaged.

Make such a denial! And what of the fact that he could wish to do so, – that he should think of such falsehood, and even meditate on the perpetration of such cowardice? He had held that young girl to his heart on that very morn-

Left *Frontispiece by Sir John Everett Millais. Outside Mrs Dale's home: the men are Crosbie and Bernard Dale; the girls are Lily and her sister.* Right *Sweet Memories, by Lionel J. Cowen, 1874. Lily Dale enjoyably making a martyr of herself*

ing. He had sworn to her, and had also sworn to himself, that she should have no reason for distrusting him. He had acknowledged most solemnly to himself that, whether for good or ill, he was bound to her; and could it be he was already calculating as to the practicability of disowning her? In doing so must he not have told himself that he was a villain? But in truth he made no such calculation. His object was to banish the subject, if it were possible to do so; to think of some answer by which he might create a doubt. It did not occur to him to tell the Countess boldly that there was no truth whatever in the report and that Miss Dale was nothing to him. But might he not skilfully laugh off the subject, even in the presence of Lady Julia? Men who were engaged did so usually, and why should not he? It was generally thought that solicitude for the lady's feelings should prevent a man from talking openly of his own engagement. Then he remembered the easy freedom with which his position had been discussed throughout the whole neighbourhood of Allington, and felt for the first time that the Dale family had been almost indelicate

[165]

in their want of reticence. 'I suppose it was done to tie me the faster,' he said to himself, as he pulled out the ends of his cravat. 'What a fool I was to come here, or indeed to go anywhere, after settling myself as I have done.' And then he went down into the drawing room.[7]

Neither of these disquisitions has as much of the untiring, hard, and unsentimental insight as he was to show later, and which he was able to show by means of this apparently easy-going technique: but the germ is there, and some of it is subtler than it looks (note the reference to 'lack of delicacy' exhibited by the Dales). So the psychological narrative in this novel is worth our attention. As with the earlier attempts of many writers, we can begin to see what he was up to, and how he was threshing about to achieve it.

No people, of course, have thought to themselves in the present moment as Crosbie is thinking to himself. In fact, the method like all others that anyone has found to represent mental experience is one of a set of different conventions: that is as true of Joyce as of others. But this is irrelevant here. Trollope was not concerned about the present moment. He was trying to suggest the present experience *as it might be considered later* and as it impinged upon future actions.

He loses something in the process, but any attempt to render mental experience loses something in the process. What he did not lose was what he most – or, at times, exclusively – wanted to do: that is, tell a continuous psychological history leading to a set of moral choices. For that, in its more sophisticated forms, his device of the psychological stream is beautifully suited. The sedateness, the gentility, the steadiness, are all deceptive. No writer was more interested in psychological drama. It is that, by the way, which makes him one of the most obsessively readable of novelists.

Along with everyone else, though, he didn't find his way to a convincing representation of mental existence. There have been plenty of attempts since. None has really worked, certainly not worked perfectly. Some have done things Trollope couldn't do, at the cost of not being able to do things he did so well. The evidence of a hundred years of artistic struggle is that there is a principle of mutual exclusion.

Trollope had many deficiencies: but if he hadn't had those deficiencies, it is arguable that his main purpose wouldn't have come off. There are limits in all art. Some attempts to ignore the Trollopian limits have brought many novels to the condition of Alexandrian poetry. Such poetry can have its place, but its place is in the history of ingenious blind alleys, not in the revelation of human nature.

19

END OF A STOIC

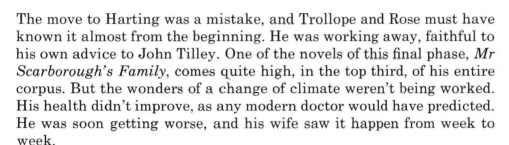

The move to Harting was a mistake, and Trollope and Rose must have known it almost from the beginning. He was working away, faithful to his own advice to John Tilley. One of the novels of this final phase, *Mr Scarborough's Family*, comes quite high, in the top third, of his entire corpus. But the wonders of a change of climate weren't being worked. His health didn't improve, as any modern doctor would have predicted. He was soon getting worse, and his wife saw it happen from week to week.

He wrote in a letter, to E.A. Freeman the historian:

> I can't sleep, willing or not willing. I can't write, as you see, because my hand is paralysed [most of his letters at this period are in his niece's handwriting and were dictated to her]. I can't sit easily because of a huge truss I wear, and now has come this damnable asthma! But still I am very good to look at, as I am not afraid to die I am as happy as other people.[1]

That was the front he could put on, stoically, even jauntily, with people who didn't know him well. He and Rose had not many visitors at Harting, but those who came did not find him depressing. His spirits could still be high. He was living in countrified comfort, not in country gentleman's splendour as at Waltham, but with two large cottages knocked into one, a housekeeper and a couple of maids, some acres of land, a cow and poultry and a garden to potter in. But the two of them had not much to occupy them. They went to church, but Trollope, in spite of the Barchester books, was not addicted to liturgical religion or, one sometimes suspects underneath his reticence, to formal religion of any kind.

To those he could trust – there were not many, Rose, Tom, his son Henry, perhaps old friends like John Tilley – he made no secret of his being sad. He longed for the Garrick, tea, whist, badinage. He could not walk far. The hours hung heavy.

A year or so before they moved to Harting, he made his will. He was not the man to leave business unfinished. The will itself was simple. Apart from minor bequests, his estate was left in trust to his wife. After her death it was to be divided equally between the two sons: Henry, the elder son, was to be his literary executor.

The estate itself proved to be worth just over twenty-five thousand pounds (the future of the literary property ignored, which was, since death duties were small, the ordinary practice of this period). This seems less than might be expected, but one has to multiply by between six and ten to get an approximate 1990s equivalent. Victorian writers did not, in absolute terms, make big fortunes. Dickens left ninety thousand, but almost exactly half of this accrued from his two final suicidal lecture tours, one in the United States, the last in England. George Eliot's capital is harder to estimate, because of her arrangements with Lewes, but it was slightly greater than Trollope's, something like thirty thousand. Wilkie Collins' was much less, only twelve thousand, which really did not provide for his miscellaneous and irregular dependants: it is difficult to understand how he left so little, since his earning powers per book in the sixties were much higher than those of any other writer, Dickens excepted. He was a shrewd businessman, as all the great Victorians were, and managed to extract about twice Trollope's price when Trollope was at his peak.

Trollope's estate did not do as handsomely by his sons as he must have wished. This was simply because Rose lived into her mid-nineties. The evidence suggests that she used the trust income competently, provided for herself, and distributed some to each of her sons. There would, after the desert phase which followed his death, have been a steady trickle of literary earnings. In the twentieth century he was never so completely out of circulation as has often been assumed. The trust income, plus literary earnings, must have given a minimum of two thousand pounds per annum throughout Rose's long life. Henry survived to eighty himself, but only had nine years of the trust's full value. His brother Fred had died long before, leaving a large family. Henry had a son and daughter, both childless, so that the English branch died out.

The testamentary matter in the preceding paragraphs has been included as a propitiation to Trollope's shade. He would not have approved of leaving it out. It was no doubt a satisfaction to him at Harting that his

Opposite *Sir John Everett Millais, self portrait, 1883.* 'Altogether he drew from my tales eighty-seven drawings, and I do not think that more conscientious work was ever done by man ... I have had my own early ideas impressed indelibly on my memory by the excellence of his delineations.' Autobiography. Overleaf *The Private View at the Royal Academy, by William Powell Frith, 1881. Trollope is fourth from the left*

financial affairs were tidy and all contingencies looked after. It may have been another satisfaction that at Harting they were living well within his income.

If so, that was about the only satisfaction that existence there could bring him. In the closing years, he was, with intermissions, stoical but no more than stoical. He still wrote letters, by modern standards many. After his stroke, most of them were taken down by his niece. His own handwriting, like his physical condition, was older than that of a man just over sixty-five. Occasionally he wrote letters in a reflective mood, as though he were tired of the bluffness and false crudity of the auto-biography. There is an interesting one to Lady Pollock about money as a motive for writers – 'but also duty: which comprehends such excellence as the workman may attain, though it be attained at the expense of profit.'[2] In the autobiography, he could not bring himself to say anything like that, even mildly to his own credit.

For the most part, in 1881 and 1882, he withdrew himself into the solace of his family. As old men often feel, he did not want the company of those he had not known for a lifetime. How much he talked to his wife, we do not know, but we do know that she was watching him more and more anxiously, realizing that Harting was doing him harm. He wrote often to Tom, who had lost all his money but in his seventies was working sturdily as a newspaper correspondent in Rome (he lived to be eighty-four). Trollope wrote often also to his son Henry.

These letters are, in a restrained fashion, touching. Trollope had been a little, not excessively, disappointed in Henry. He was now in his mid-thirties, and Trollope still hoped that he would reach some sort of distinction. Trollope kept giving knowledgeable literary advice. He used all the influence he possessed – untypically, since, though he understood personal manoeuvres, he did not like them – to get Henry elected to the Athenaeum. He was disproportionately elated (it was one of the happiest days of his old age) when that duly happened. Two hundred votes to four, the largest majority anyone could remember![3] Trollope had been 'awfully nervous'![4] He retired to the cardoom, like a playwright parading out-side the theatre on a first night. People came and told him the news. Since Henry was going to be elected by an enormous majority, this anxiety was, of course, quite unrealistic, but all through that closing year he was brooding over his son.

He made forty-eight dozen of claret over to him (1874 Beycheville and Léoville: none of the Trollopes were heavy drinkers, and Trollope him-

Opposite *Dinner at Haddo House* (detail), *by Alfred Edward Emslie, 1884. In the foreground are Lady Aberdeen and, on her right, Gladstone*

self drank almost no spirits, but he kept his cultivated taste in wine). That transference was a symbol of life going on.[5]

Most of all, though, Trollope wanted Henry to visit him. In this Henry, though he did go once or twice, seems to have been remiss. We cannot tell the circumstances. Henry got married shortly after his father's death, and in that final year of Trollope's life spent a good deal of time

The Trollopes' house at Harting

touring in France. In just one of Trollope's letters to his wife, there is a cry of fierce impatience.[6]

Trollope had a scheme that he and Henry might share a flat in London, so that Trollope could spend the winter there. He was convinced that he would be better and less depressed in London[7] – and he needed his son near him. Nothing came of this.

He was thinking often about death. This is shown most nakedly in letters which have not yet been published. In the Bradford Booth edition, there are just over nine hundred Trollope letters: there remain over two hundred unpublished. These range in date from 1839 to the last months of Trollope's life.[8]

The more significant of these letters are nearly all to his brother Tom. Trollope turned to him as he turned to Henry. Most of these consist of fragments, single pages recovered from what must have been three- or four-page letters. He and Tom had become closer as they grew old, and to his brother Trollope didn't pretend. In some way, these terse fragments are the most unveiled in all Trollope's correspondence. As in some

[170]

examples: to Tom in 1880: 'It sometimes will take a man five years to die. As soon as I have not a book to finish, I shall go.'

To Tom, fragment, probably 1881: 'I take the fact to be that I am ill here and should be well in London. It is a bore.'

To Tom, fragment, probably 1882: 'I certainly do not play much at Harting.'

Postal deliveries late in Trollope's life. Compare the rough-and-ready methods when he started at the Post Office

To an unnamed recipient:

Dear friend, I cannot be in here both Thursday and Friday. I will see Dr Murrell on Friday. What I fear is that I shall be told to live altogether in town – or anywhere but here. I have taken a house and furnished it, and at my age it would be very mischievous to make another moving: and the more so as this place suits my wife. There is only one easy way out of the trouble that I can see.

[Almost certainly not written to an intimate friend. Note the absence of complaint about Harting, always present when he wrote to Tom. Rose didn't wish him to stay there, as became clear a few months later.]

To Tom, fragment, probably 1882: [Here the writing, not always easy to decipher in these last letters, is unusually difficult.] '– have come on one of which I have often spoken to you, in which I should know that it were better that I were dead.'

Even the moods of an ill aging man aren't permanent. In May 1882 and again in August, escorted and half nursed by his niece, he made trips to

Ireland. Irrepressibly he was refreshing his memory for another novel. This was *The Land Leaguers*, which was never to be published. For the first time, his creative powers were demonstrably failing. There is a certain shapeliness, though, that the last novel should return to the setting of the first.

He came back to Harting, and a doctor wouldn't have needed to take many looks at him. With her usual sense, Rose took him to London. It might have been better if that had been done two years before. He would have had Henry within call, and doctors (though they couldn't do much in the 1880s for his blood pressure, any more than they could for Dickens's). Rose took a suite in the old Garlands Hotel in Suffolk Street, at the Trafalgar Square end of Pall Mall. The hotel was a fashionable meeting-place of the late nineteenth century, and at the end of the street, near the stage door of the Haymarket Theatre. Trollope managed to have a fair round of social life. He went to the Garrick and enjoyed himself. He even

Left *Christening Sunday, by James Charles, 1887. This was the church at Harting which the Trollopes attended.* Right *Garlands Hotel, 1933. No longer a hotel in 1991. The stage door of the Haymarket Theatre is on the left*

went down to Somerset to stay with E.A. Freeman, who had a singular gift for being warmly and cosily friendly with men he had once insulted on paper. He had done this to Trollope and exactly the same to Charles Kingsley.

Back in London, Trollope dined with Alexander Macmillan, another close friend, and next night he and Rose went to dine with John Tilley and his daughter. Tilley, an inveterate marrier, had just buried his third wife. His daughter was keeping house for him in St George's Square, rather an unfashionable neighbourhood, one would have thought, for a retired Chief Secretary of the Post Office with a handsome pension. Pimlico had never been smart as the developers had once hoped.

The river lay at the end of the square, and the houses were only forty years old. The Tilleys lived in theirs very much as Trollope's parents had once lived in Keppel Street. As the Trollopes had done, they had their dining room on the ground floor; and that night, entertaining Trollope and Rose, they went upstairs after dinner to the drawing room.

There Trollope – the others remembered him later as being unusually hilarious and excited – told how, earlier that evening, he had had from his window at Garlands an altercation with a German band. After which one of the Tilleys did some reading aloud, in the high Victorian domestic manner. The book chosen for reading was the latest popular success, Anstey's *Vice Versa*. They were vastly amused, Trollope emitting the explosive laughter that had battered round the Post Office and the Garrick Club. *Vice Versa* appealed to the contemporary taste for the facetious (the soul of a middle-aged man finds itself in the body of a young boy), and to them all nothing could be more uproarious. The creator of some of the subtlest comedy of the age thought it far funnier than anything he had written. It was a cheerful family party, like many they had known. Then some of the laughter ceased. It can't have taken long for Rose to see that her husband had tilted over in his chair. He couldn't speak. He was paralysed down his right side.

In hospital he lay for nearly a month. *The Times* published bulletins. He recovered enough to limp once or twice about his room. He never spoke again. When he was conscious, he knew what was happening to him. He couldn't communicate. It was a specially lonely death.

There is a temptation which has been too much for people trying to tell Trollope's life story. It is to finish with the closing words of his autobiography: 'Now I stretch out my hand, and from the further shore I bid adieu to all who have cared to read any among the many words that I have written.'

It was more rhetorical than Trollope's usual tone to finish like that. He was going to live some more years and write a good many more words, some excellent. Still, in the peculiar tone of the autobiography, it is per-

*Alexander Macmillan, the younger of the two brothers who
founded the family firm. He was a close friend of Trollope, who
dined with him the night before the final stroke. Painting by
Sir Hubert Herkomer, 1887*

haps all right. For us to leave him there, though, seems quite impermis-
sibly sentimental. He was far from being a sentimental man. He would
accept the reason why we are interested in him now. And for us, of
course, the story didn't finish on 6 December 1882.

We probably know as much about him now as we are likely to. That is,
there are a few gaps in the factual history, and a few questions which an
historically minded scholar would like to be answered. But even if this
happens, it is reasonably certain that it won't alter our impression much.

That impression will depend on our own temperament, and the way in which we interpret and respond to his. For some of us, he will remain one of the most admirable characters in literary history, where experience shows it isn't easy to be such a character. The reason for this is simple. A writer, particularly an exploratory psychological writer such as Trollope, has to live on close terms with the blacker – including the worse – side of his own nature. It isn't true of other creative persons. Einstein, brooding on the fundamental concept of physics, could suppress, and suppress for the rest of his life, the parts of his nature which he thought debased. Dostoevsky, writing *The Brothers Karamazov* (which Einstein thought the greatest of all works of literature), couldn't do anything of the kind. It takes unusual moral fibre for a writer to make himself into a decent man. Trollope did it.

He belongs to a category along with Chekhov and Walter Scott, straightforward on the outside, complicated and sometimes maze-like within. There is nothing surprising, though there is a good deal inpenetrable, about this, and most people who have studied his personal life have discovered a lot of common ground.

The history of his books has been much more dramatic. He died nearly a hundred years ago. Immediately after death, there was a precipitous slump, in reputation and everything else. Something similar happens to nearly all writers, but this was catastrophic. The autobiography did much harm. It would have done harm at any period, but it couldn't have been worse timed. The aesthetic climate of the eighties and nineties couldn't tolerate it, either when he was telling hard truths, even less when he was telling what seemed to them his brutal apologies – which was really an elaborate self-depreciation and a kind of arrogance.

However, the anti-Trollope swing would have happened anyway. It was visible before the autobiography. He was already being written off in the obituaries. He had only been semi-tolerated by the rank-and-file literary world through most of his career. Proust said Balzac was read and admired only by the people he wrote about, retired colonels, engineers, priests. Something of the same was Trollope's condition in his lifetime. He had eminent supporters, but usually outside the opinion formers.

Cardinal Newman was the last supporter in Trollope's lifetime and one of the most perceptive. But it takes a great deal to submerge good books. In a subdued fashion, some of the more famous began to be re-issued. This was already happening before the turn of the century. Some independent intellectuals, a few of them professionally occupied with literature, a great many not, were discovering Trollope. Those who lived into the thirties were proud of themselves (like premature Dickensians). Some of them, when old, used to say that, as young men, Trollope was the novelist for them, just as Ibsen was the playwright, a combination which bears looking at. Rose Trollope was alive and intellectually capable, and

Left *Tom Trollope*. Right *Trollope at 67*

young literary journalists like Desmond MacCarthy used to go and talk to her. There was a small but not negligible Trollope underground. More re-issues. Sales small, but presumably just worth publishers' time. Prices of the first editions low. Trollope not an o.k. name. In advanced circles Meredith, though it is difficult to believe, was called the greatest of all novelists. Yet anyone with a really acute ear to the ground might have guessed just before the First World War that Trollope was coming back. Escott's biography, amiable but undistinguished and also inaccurate, did a certain amount of good.

After the war, and before Sadleir's work, the Trollope revival was gaining momentum. This was forty years after his death, unusually late: but from that time it has, with minor inflections on the curve, been irreversible. Sadleir's bibliography gives the price of first editions, which tell one part of the story. His biography, though curious in literary taste, was just what the time required. In the thirties the American scholars were getting to work, often more thoroughly than Sadleir. Trollope was being read again, by a large public. The underground emerged overground.

The war is sometimes given the credit for Trollope's present popularity. Actually, the wave was evident years before. Julian Blackwood had begun to publish a complete edition of the novels. It has also been said

[176]

that Trollope was read in England during the war just for reasons of escape and nostalgia. This has been discussed in chapter 13. It is worth noting that, in wartime, at precisely the same period as Harold Macmillan and Bernard Montgomery were re-reading Trollope at different spots in North Africa, Booth and his school in Los Angeles were starting the most accomplished Trollope studies yet known.

That wasn't nostalgia, or if so it was a nostalgia of a peculiarly rarefied kind. Most of those scholars hadn't ancestral connections with Trollope's characters or Trollope's society. They thought he was a fine writer: and because they could see him without any of the English mists, they saw him with fresh eyes, as he must have wanted the books to be read when he first published them.

Since the early forties, nearly all the most penetrating academic work on Trollope has been done in America, much of it in California, where the scholarly periodical *The Trollopian*, later called *Nineteenth Century Fiction*, was initiated.

None of this would have disconcerted Trollope. He was, as has been shown, one of the least chauvinistic of men. He actually remarked, in the letter in which he said that patriotism isn't the most overriding value:

> I was thinking today that nature intended me for an American rather than an Englishman. I think I should have made a better American yet I hold it higher to be a bad Englishman, as I am, than a good American, as I am not.[12]

No one has ever yet quite disentangled what he meant by those gnomic remarks. Yet it is a pleasing irony that he should have found his best and most understanding critics in America.

When one reads those critics, one feels that his work is at last beginning to be understood. It will be a long time before their criticism passes into general currency. But it has cleared away much obtuseness. His art has been established at last, more firmly than in his own time. And that will go on for as long as we can now foresee. Maybe this is not an unsatisfactory place to stop, and we can remember that Trollope himself stopped waving his hand long ago.

NOTES TO THE TEXT

SOURCES

References in the notes are to the editions mentioned below, except when otherwise specified. Abbreviated reference symbols are in parentheses before the title.

1 PRIMARY

The primary sources about Trollope – except for his own writings – are scanty. By far the greatest part of what has been written about him derives from the same limited material.

(*Auto*) *An Autobiography*, Anthony Trollope (2 vols, London, 1883. References in the present work are to the edition reissued with an introduction by Bradford A. Booth, by the University of California Press, 1947). This book has been mentioned frequently in the present study. It is one of the oddest documents in literary history. It is, in its own strange way, a beautiful and moving work of art, a mixture of extravagant self-depreciation and subterranean pride. In principle it tells a good many truths about him, but in detail has to be read with a fair degree of suspicion. In terms of fact, there are considerable lacunae and a number of errors.

(*Letters*) *Letters of Anthony Trollope*, edited by Bradford A. Booth (London, 1951). Trollope didn't keep many letters to himself, and, apart from business correspondence, wrote few, by Victorian standards. Of those few, a large proportion have been lost, notably many to his mother and to his son Fred. The Booth collection amounts to less than a thousand – compare Dickens's many thousand. The Trollope letters are not often directly rewarding, though they yield something to attentive readers.

The index to the O.U.P., London, 1951 edition is worse than inadequate, and to use the letters effectively requires a good memory.

Letters so far unpublished. Since the Booth edition, a considerable number of letters have been added to the Morris L. Parrish collection at Princeton. The present writer has had the privilege of studying these (see Preface). They consist of 205 letters and 31 fragments. As mentioned in ch. 19, the fragments, particularly those written near the end of Trollope's life, are unusually interesting.

Enquiries have been made to Sir Anthony Trollope, Trollope's great-grandson, in Sydney, N.S.W. No further unpublished matter of any kind appears to exist now in Australia.

(*WIR*) *What I Remember*, Thomas Adolphus Trollope (3 vols, London, 1887–9). These are the memoirs of Trollope's brother Tom, written when he was nearing eighty. They say little about Trollope, and nothing specially illuminating. On the other hand, they are the best source for the family and the family background. Allowance has to be made for Tom's worshipping attachment to his mother. Allowance has also to be made for Tom's own personality. He probably wasn't quite the simple, straightforward, unassuming character that he presents.

2 SECONDARY SOURCES–NEAR CONTEMPORARY
(FET) *Frances Trollope: Her Life and Literary Work (from George III to Victoria)*, Frances Eleanor Trollope (2 vols, London, 1895). Frances Eleanor Trollope – Fanny – was Tom's second wife, and a sister of Ellen Ternan, Dickens's mistress. Fanny never met Mrs Trollope Sr, who was dead by the time Fanny was sent to Florence by Tom's brother and sister-in-law as a deliberate manoeuvre. They were determined to provide someone to look after Tom now both his mother

and first wife were dead. This happened. Fanny was nearly thirty years younger than Tom, but they married, and happily. She was a clever woman, as all three Ternan girls were, and had a genuine literary talent. Her views, however, were absorbed lock, stock and barrel from Tom, and the book, though lively and intelligent, is largely an exercise in vicarious heroine-worship. She admired Trollope's novels, but as in Tom's memoirs, there is little about him here.

(Escott) *Anthony Trollope: His Work, Associations, and Literary Originals,* T.H.S. Escott (London, 1913). Escott, as a young literary journalist with social connections, became intimate with Trollope in the final years. Escott had some insight, and came to understand Trollope well. The book is slapdash, and a good many factual statements are incorrect, but it is by no means negligible. It gives the only picture we have, from a first-hand observer, of how Trollope behaved to a close friend whom he trusted.

(Gregory) *An Autobiography,* Sir William Gregory (London, 1894). A single but significant mention of Trollope at Harrow. Interesting in itself.

A Diary, William Allingham (London, 1907). Several mentions of Trollope.

Autobiography. Alfred Austin (London, 1911). Austin knew Tom better than Trollope, but there are shrewd comments on both. Whatever Austin's poetry was like, he was an exceptionally able back-room political operator, and gave Lord Salisbury advice – usually good – about personal appointments.

Life of Lord Houghton. T. Wemyss Reid (2 vols, London, 1890). Only one letter of Trollope's, but the book suggests something of the circles Trollope knew in later life. Lord Houghton was better known as Monckton-Milnes, one of the more amusing if disreputable of Victorian grandees.

(Whiting) *Kate Field,* Lillian Whiting (London, 1899). Not much about Trollope, but innocently revelatory of Kate Field. Has not often been read with enough attention.

3 SOURCES OF RECORD
Usual archives for family wills, etc.

(*Critical Heritage*) *Anthony Trollope, The Critical Heritage*, edited by Donald Smalley (London, 1969). One of the valuable 'Critical Heritage' series. It gives a wide selection of reviews of Trollope's books from the first novel onwards. If this apparatus had been available to Sadleir and other early Trollope scholars, it would have saved many false emphases.

Trollope's business papers. These are kept at the Bodleian Library, Oxford. Nothing has been discovered which substantially modifies his own account of his business affairs.

(POR) Post Office Records. Previously, these seem not to have been seriously examined. Hence a good many mistakes and some false allegations have survived by default. The Post Office Records tell much about Trollope's official career, and contain surprises (see Ch. 15). They might yield more, on further examination.

4 SECONDARY SOURCES – NON-CONTEMPORARY
(*Commentary*) *A Commentary*, Michael Sadleir (London, 1927). Scholarly and well-informed on Trollope's publishing history and bibliography. Not scholarly about his Post Office career, where appropriate material was not identified. Not scholarly, also, about Trollope's literary reception in his lifetime.

These are serious defects, and the critical and personal judgments are erratic. However, the book is admirably written, and was a major event in a new Trollope epoch. It had a decisive influence on Bradford A. Booth.

(Stebbins) *The Trollopes: The Chronicle of a Writing Family*, Lucy Poate Stebbins and Richard Poate Stebbins (London, 1946). This mother and son collaboration is perhaps the most eccentric work which bears on Trollope's biography. The Stebbins unearthed more facts, and useful facts, than any other biographers. They were writing about the Trollope family as a whole, and became devoted to Tom, and even more to his mother. They were singularly hostile to Trollope himself, so much so that their accuracy – often rigorous – deserted them. They made some attacks on him without any basis at all – as about the falsity of his claim to have initiated the pillar-box, and his hypocrisy about anonymous publication. These attacks won't stand examination, and have been disposed of.

Anthony Trollope, Bradford A. Booth (Indiana and London, 1958). Reliable, like all Booth's work, but not quite the definitive book he might have produced. More a series of reflections than a composed biography. A good deal of time was spent in demolishing Stebbins.

(Pope Hennessy) *Anthony Trollope*, James Pope Hennessy (London, 1971). The fullest biographical account yet written. Not specially good on the novels, very sensible on the personality. Admirable on Trollope's travels. Pope Hennessy knew Ireland and the West Indies intimately, and followed all Trollope's journeys. This biography is now, for most purposes, more useful than Sadleir's.

5 CRITICISM

Until twenty years ago, there was little good criticism of Trollope. Since then, some excellent works have appeared.

Anthony Trollope, A Critical Study, A.O.J. Cockshutt (London, 1955). Still the best English effort, but a maddening book. Some original insights, some deep, which Cockshutt didn't follow through. One part of the book is distorted by religious predelections.

Trollope, Artist and Moralist, Ruth apRoberts (London, 1971). In a good many ways the best yet, not only about Trollope, but the theory of the realistic novel in general. She deals with Trollope's religious attitudes more wisely than anyone else has done, and has new things to say about his psychological gifts. Essential reading.

The Changing World of Anthony Trollope, Robert M. Polhemus (California, 1968). Very good. Full of understanding of Trollope's literary temperament. Ruth apRoberts has criticized the book sharply for errors of judgment about the Victorian church, with which he is not at home. From this side of the Atlantic, both she and Polhemus stand out as two of the ablest critics who have written on Trollope.

The Trollopian, and *Nineteenth-Century Fiction*. This is actually the same academic publication with a change of name. It has contained valuable articles on Trollope by, among a number of others, John H. Hagan (1958–9), Jerome Thale (1960), David A. Aitken (1966–74), Roger L. Slakey (1973).

6 BACKGROUND READING

Trollope's novels

As a counsel of perfection, other major novelists of the 19th century, not only in English. It is a help to have Trollope's contemporaries in mind.

As another counsel of perfection, all or anything about the 19th century that comes one's way. Two works which are particularly useful in understanding some social areas in Trollope's novels are: *The Victorian Church*, W.O. Chadwick (2 vols, London, 1966–70). Essential reading for the Barchester novels – and *Life of Robert Marquis of Salisbury*, Lady Gwendoline Cecil (4 vols, London, 1921–32). Instructive about what life in a great political house, comparable with the Pallisers but on the conservative side, was like.

NOTES

1: BORN A GENTLEMAN
1 Anthony Trollope, novelist, 1815–82, is referred to as *Trollope* tout court, throughout. His family and friends called him Anthony (a very few, Tony): but we don't know him well enough for that, and it gives the impression of heartiness and simplicity which it is one of the intentions of this book to dispel.

His eldest brother is called Tom throughout, his father Mr Trollope, his mother Mrs Trollope, his wife Rose.
2 Not so ebullient, perhaps. Dostoevsky Sr was as morose as Mr Trollope and an alcoholic into the bargain (see Leonid Grossman, *Dostoevsky*, London, 1975).
3 *WIR* 1, p. 5.
4 *Auto,* p. 1, p. 34, p. 244.
5 *Auto,* pp. 32–4. See also *Last Chronicle of Barset*, ch. 15, as example of fictional reference.
6 Though even Trollope was sometimes put off by the West, *Letters*, no. 167 (to Kate Field).
7 *Last Chronicle of Barset*, ch. 24.

8 *The Duke's Children*, ch. 8, called (sardonically) 'He is a Gentleman'.
9 *Last Chronicle of Barset*, ch. 83.
10 The present writer is speaking from personal experience. (Changes of usage get a passing notice in C.P. Snow's *The Masters*.)
11 It would, as a rule, mean that they were ordained in the Anglican Church.
12 *Auto*, p. 78. He also says that he had had 'no peculiar intimacy with any clergyman,' which was overdoing it considerably.
13 *WIR* 1, p. 296.
14 *Auto*, p. 27. *WIR* also comments on his great physical strength.
15 *WIR* 1, pp. 62–8. Incidentally, Mr Trollope's uncle long outlived him.
16 Compare Stebbins, p. 15.
17 Compare Escott, throughout. Also her own biographer, FET. It may seem over-suspicious to remark that neither had ever met her.
18 Robert Browning, letter to his wife in 1843 – 'I do hope, Ba, you won't receive that vulgar,

pushing woman.' Later the Brownings entered Mrs Trollope's house on friendly terms, with just detectable reserve. They admired Trollope himself much more than the Mrs Trollope-Tom combination.

2: ODD CHILD OUT

1 *Auto*, p. 12. *WIR* 1, p. 58. Mr Trollope combined this fanatical industry-cum-discipline with an unstoppable consumption of calomel.

2 Winchester, like other major English schools, is well documented, and the accounts of the Trollope brothers can be checked from school histories and similar records.

3 *WIR* 1, p. 77.

4 Tom had read, after Trollope's death, the *Autobiography*, years before he wrote his own memoirs. He didn't correct this singular story. It does seem exaggerated, on someone's part.

5 Trollope pays an affectionate tribute to Tom, on the other hand, in the *Autobiography*.

6 It is fair to say that, at the end of his life (see ch. 19), Trollope was writing intimate letters to Tom, and one may infer that he received something similar in return.

7 *Domestic Manners of the Americans*, chs 3–5, gives a high-spirited, dismissive account. Stebbins, which generally shares the heroine-worship of Escott and FET, is slightly more critical and contains the best continuous narrative.

8 He did know his bills at Winchester were not being paid, and that his pocket money (a shilling a week) was stopped, which all the other Collegers, and college servants, also knew. *Auto*, p. 8.

9 How this general pattern of imbibing took hold is still something of a mystery. They didn't smoke cigarettes, it is true, and they didn't drink so much spirits. But their dosage of drugs or medicines would seem to us lethal.

10 FET 1, pp. 171–2.

11 *Last Chronicle of Barset*, ch. 41.

3: WALKING TO SCHOOL

1 Alban Hall, where Tom was sent, was not even specially inexpensive. Mr Trollope appears to have chosen it on purely political grounds. The Principal was a staunch Whig. He also happened to disapprove of Winchester and Wykenhamists.

2 He admitted himself that he would probably have won a Fellowship. *Auto*, p. 9.

3 As a rough approximation, split around the latitudinarian middle, Tories high church, Whigs low. There were, of course, exceptions, the most spectacular being Mr Gladstone, a devout high churchman.

4 *Auto*, p. 8. Note the '*of course*'.

5 Actually, about three miles. The Harrow environment has changed out of visual recognition since Trollope's time. That path through country lanes would now go across playing-fields. Harrow Weald is untraceable, except in terms of vague locality. The site of Julians can be established.

Trollope was not always alone on those walks to school, as his own account suggests. Frequently he picked up a companion en route.

6 Gregory, p. 35.

7 Gregory was an attractive character, and it is a pity that that is his one reference to Trollope, whom he later knew well. Gregory ran through a considerable part of his family fortune, but was looked after by friends and managed to stabilize himself. He may have been a part-original for Phineas Finn. Religion apart, he had a good many of Finn's attributes. Like other Ascendancy squires, he became antipathetic to his own (Tory) party's policy on Ireland, and a strong supporter of Tenants' Rights. This, though he had been a Tory M.P. and got the governorship of Ceylon as a consolation prize. When he and Trollope were both old, he had become much more liberal on Ireland than the one-time liberal candidate.

8 Stebbins, p. 53.

9 Personal reminiscence of present writer.

10 *Auto*, p. 36.

11 *Domestic Manners of the Americans*, ch. 30–4.

12 *Auto*, p. 14. *WIR* 1, pp. 218–35, insists that Harrow Weald was not so derelict as described by Trollope.

13 The new house was the original of Orley Farm, and represented as such in the first illustrations of the novel.

14 Who also died of TB, at the age of 17.

15 A number of theoretically liberal English people, who might have thought themselves Utopians, went to the United States *c*. 1830–50, thinking they expected the best, and disillusioned before they arrived. Dickens is an example. Compare Western visitors to the Soviet Union a hundred years later.

16 Compare the benevolent activity of Mr Toogood in *The Last Chronicle of Barset*.

4: OCCUPATION FOR A YOUNG MAN

1 *Auto*, pp. 24–5. FET 1, pp. 205 et seq gives a much fuller description, largely based on Mrs Trollope's letters to Tom. Tom himself, with his usual luck, missed the worst of it. He was tutoring in London.

2 He stayed only six weeks, and didn't learn much French – nor teach much Classics.

3 Mrs Trollope had a close friend, Mrs Clayton Freeling, whose father-in-law was the Secretary (i.e., top permanent official) of the Post Office.

4 *Auto*, p. 50.

5 *Auto*, p. 50, loc. cit. The whole passage is among the most revelatory that Trollope wrote.

6 There are certain kinds of experience – occasionally dramatic, like Dostoevsky watching the firing squad, occasionally quite pedestrian, like John Eames walking away from Lily Dale – the tone of which no writer, if he had not felt the experience himself, could invent. Others, including some spectacular kinds, are quite easy to invent.

7 *WIR* 1, p. 179. Trollope, *Auto*, p. 36–7, says that even in daydreams he couldn't think of himself as six feet high.

8 *Varieties of Temperament, Varieties of Physique*, by W.H. Sheldon.

9 His Latin was probably better than he admitted. Later on, he read Latin authors for pleasure.

10 Tom made the same complaint. Also William Gregory, vehemently, who had been top of the school at Harrow. Also Edmund Yates from Highgate, a less elevated establishment. Alfred Austin, who went to catholic schools (one of which, Stonyhurst, he much disliked) had an appreciably more sensible academic education.

11 *Essays in the History of Publishing* (London, 1974), see 'Latin for Yesterday', R.M. Ogilvie, pp. 219–44.

12 Letters, no. 1, to Richard Bentley, 24 May, 1835.

5: SURVIVAL IN THE PUBLIC SERVICE

1 i.e., the chief Permanent official, known as the Secretary. The political head was known as the Postmaster General, and was a member of the Government though not normally in the Cabinet.

2 *Auto*, p. 34, loc. cit., and frequently throughout his novels.

3 There is some material in the *Autobiography of Sir Henry Taylor* (London, 1885).

4 Not much has yet been published about the Victorian Civil Service, though a serious historical treatment is being prepared by Oxford scholars. Compare in passing C.P. Snow, 'Dickens and the Circumlocution Office' in *Dickens 1970* (London, 1970).

5 He was appointed, aged 24, at the high initial salary of £350, rising rapidly to £600. This seems to have been a recognition of his impressive personality and his literary promise. He had done no administrative work whatever and had expressed no interest in it.

6 This is distinctly too grudging. The verse-drama wasn't a good form for him – or for anyone else since. But in our time he might have written excellent historical novels.

6: THE BEST YEARS OF ONE'S LIFE

1 *Auto,* p. 37.

2 *WIR* 1, p. 370, FET 1, p. 291.

3 *Auto*, pp. 47–8. Even here, though, there is a melancholy note. One of the three young men in the Tramp Society was Trollope's equivalent of Browning's Waring. The other two loved him, and hoped for his future. But Browning's Waring became – believe it or not – Prime Minister of New Zealand. Trollope's friend came to a bad end, and is referred to as W–A for that reason.

4 *Auto*, p. 43.

5 Compare his behaviour in lodgings in *The Small House at Allington*, when he is as impecunious as the young Trollope, with his more exalted (though risky) flirtation with Miss Demolines in *The Last Chronicle of Barset*, after he has come into Lord de Guest's legacy.

6 *Auto*, pp. 40–1.

7 *Auto*, p. 44.

8 *Commentary*, pp. 121–2. Sadleir was being over-delicate, and was taking his period's view of Victorian behaviour.

9 Escott, p. 27. As a matter of bleak history, the *Autobiography*, not for the only time, makes the worst of a bad job. In her fairy godmother rôle, Mrs Trollope gave parties where Trollope must have met young women. It is disconcerting, in the light of the *Autobiography*'s outburst, to discover that he visited his mother in Paris and had a lively social time.

10 This becomes clear from his transformation when he had a modicum of success in Ireland.

11 Compare *Winter Thoughts About Summer Impressions*, Dostoevsky's western travelogue.

12 Pope Hennessy, ch. 5, section 3.

13 *Auto*, p. 45.

14 In the literal sense, it was certainly not true. He kept both a diary and a commonplace book, the latter full of reflections on literature (see Bradford A. Booth, *Anthony Trollope*, pp. 135 et seq.).

15 See note 6 to ch. 4.

16 Apparently these posts (as surveyors' clerks) were considered somewhat socially demeaning.

17 Not his first patron, Sir Francis Freeling, but Colonel Maberley, considerably less well disposed.

7: SEA-CHANGE

1 *Auto*, p. 57.

2 For description and evocation of Trollope's Irish stay, Pope Hennessy is much the best source. The author wrote his book in Banagher, and was by origin Irish – a direct descendant of the Pope Hennessy who was certainly one of the starting points, and probably the main one, for the character of Phineas Finn.

3 Escott, p. 144.
4 Letter to Tom Trollope, 1849.
5 *Letters,* no. 671, 7 October 1877.
6 *Framley Parsonage,* chs 26–77.
This impression of Rose Trollope was formed before the photograph was discovered. See p. 63. At least the photograph of Rose in middle age doesn't contradict what has been suggested in chapter 7.

8: BUILDING A CHARACTER
1 One does a good deal more than wonder.
2 *Auto*, pp. 57–8.
3 *Commentary*, pp. 141–51.
4 Pope Hennessy, ch. 8, for the physical environment.
5 Tilley was actually two years older.
6 Tom copied his mother here as elsewhere. He wrote travel books, as she did, and followed suit with novels. His own genuine interest was in history.
7 *Auto*, p. 62.
8 Dostoevsky had finished his first novel, *Poor Folk,* four months before. That same night, a summer night in Petersburg, he read it aloud to Grigorich and the poet Nekrasov. Enthusiastically, they took the manuscript to Belinsky, who, though young, was the most influential critic in Russia. He was already seriously ill, but read it the same day. Within hours he was telling Dostoevsky what a gigantic gift he possessed, and how he mustn't waste it.
   The difference between these two receptions carries certain lessons. Some encouragement at this stage might have made a difference to Trollope's career.
9 *Auto*, pp. 62–3.
10 *Critical Heritage*, pp. 546–52. Seven reviews are quoted, all but one favourable.
11 *Auto*, p. 63.
12 *Auto*, pp. 64–5.
13 A good example is Julian Hawthorne, son of Nathaniel. A passage from *Impressions and Criticisms* (Boston, 1887) is quoted in *Commentary*, pp. 337–9.
14 Escott, p. 171.
15 Sydney Smith, Anglican clergyman, wit, favourite guest at Holland House, was one of the most attractive characters of the 19th century.

9: ARRIVAL
1 Stebbins attempts to dismiss Trollope's responsibility for this innovation. But it is all quite clear in the Post Office records. See *The Letter-Box* (London, 1969) by Jean Young Farrugia, Assistant Curator of the National Postal Museum.

She has produced a scholarly treatment on the whole subject. Stebbins has a curious bias against Trollope, and this is one of the most glaring examples of it.
   After Trollope wrote his first suggestion (November 1851) the Post Office took nearly a year to erect the first boxes in Jersey. They were declared a success within a month of their appearance. Pillar boxes were almost immediately ordered for England, the first in Carlisle. Trollope himself arranged the sites for three in Gloucester.
2 See *Transatlantic Crossing*, an anthology of 19th-century American views of England, edited by Walter Allen.
3 *Auto*, p. 54.
4 *Auto*, p. 81.
5 *Letters*, no. 32, 28 September 1852.
6 *Letters*, no. 38, 28 June 1855.
7 *Auto*, p. 82.
8 For example, *The Devils, Anna Karenina, Le Rouge et Le Noir.*
9 *Auto*, p. 88.
10 Trollope had the endearing habit – which was easier because of the Victorian practice of outright sales of copyright – of recording the earnings of each book with minute accuracy. His well-known balance sheet at the end of the autobiography has given pleasure to many – and did him, in foolish minds, some harm.
11 Trollope from 1857 onwards was in great demand at the circulating libraries. This didn't mean extra earnings for the books when published, but increased his potential market value.
12 Arnold, 'The Function of Criticism at the Present Time', published in *Essays in Criticism*, London, 1865.
13 As for the weight of Arnold's physique, the present writer for a long time imagined that he was as spare as, say, T.S. Eliot. He wasn't. In his sixties, he was appreciably heavier than Trollope at the same age. He weighed 17 stone (nearly 240 pounds) which probably helped towards a regrettably premature death, for at sixty-six he died in Liverpool running after a tram.

10: AT THE BISHOP'S BEDSIDE
1 *Auto*, p. 158.
2 W.O. Chadwick, *The Victorian Church*, 1, pp. 472–4.
3 Compare attempts to obtain a deanery for Charles Kingsley, as described by Susan Chitty, *Charles Kingsley* (London, 1975).

11: TIMETABLE
1 Sea sickness didn't stop him.
2 Edmund Yates, *Recollections and Experience,*

vol. 4, pp. 222–3. There is now powerful evidence that Trollope was not an easy colleague, from one of his own protests (see ch. 15).

3 *Auto*, pp. 133–4.

4 Trollope's purchases of claret show that he took good advice. He probably also had a good palate.

5 Wilkie Collins was an exception. Heavy drug-taking (see above, ch. 2, note 9) was much more common than heavy drinking. Collins combined both.

6 *Commentary*, p. 336, tells this story without attribution.

7 *Letters*, no. 76, 23 October 1858.

8 *Letters*, no. 77, 28 October 1858.

9 Dostoevsky had to dictate *The Gambler* in a few days to meet a deadline and so escape a ruinous penalty clause.

10 *Auto*, pp. 90–1.

11 *Auto*, p. 103.

12: THE GOLDEN TIME

1 Tolstoi's Collected Works run into thirty volumes. But, apart from autobiography such as *Childhood, Boyhood and Youth*, there are only three novels which are, in the ordinary sense, works of creative art – *War and Peace, Anna Karenina, Resurrection*. Not a large production for a man who lived to the age of 82. But, to make him the greatest of novelists, enough.

2 *Auto,* p. 135.

3 Stebbins attempts to denigrate this. Booth, in his *Anthony Trollope*, demolishes the Stebbins case, which is supported by no evidence whatever.

4 *Commentary*, p. 199. The anecdote has been often repeated but the origin is obscure.

5 *The West Indies and the Spanish Main* (London, 1859).

6 Trollope himself was dissatisfied with it. Actually, short of Tocqueville, no 19th-century European writer wrote more sense about the United States.

7 FET glides over this. The second Mrs Tom Trollope understood Trollope's work much better than her husband.

8 Dickens went to great lengths to conceal his relation with Ellen from the Tom Trollopes, and was satisfied that he had succeeded. Actually, they knew all about it, as did most of his acquaintances in literary London.

9 In private conversation, James Pope Hennessy was certain of this. The present author didn't question him at the time about his authority for the statement. But he had considerable contact with the art world and wasn't gullible about gossip.

10 *Auto*, p. 262.

13: TROLLOPE'S ART – I

1 *Critical Heritage,* pp. 394–427. A number of complete reviews are quoted, nearly all of them dismissive.

2 N.N. Gusev, *Recollections*. Gusev was Tolstoi's secretary during the last years of his life. Gusev's memoirs, which are exceptionally informative though starry-eyed, are not available in English. They have not been used as a source by Troyat and other biographers of Tolstoi, which is a real omission. *Excellence*, in the sentence quoted, would be better translated as 'mastery'.

3 *Critical Heritage*, pp. 467–74.

4 Harold Macmillan, private communication.

5 Lady Dorothy Macmillan, in private conversation.

6 This gave Trollope a pleasure he wasn't used to. *Auto*, pp. 122–3.

7 *Auto*, pp. 194–5.

8 'North American Review', 1883, revised and re-published in *Partial Portraits*, 1888.

9 James was jeering at the bogus scientific determinism of Zola and others.

10 *Auto*, p. 300.

11 See ch. 18.

14: A HUMAN RELATION

1 Lillian Whiting's pious and reverend biography has its own simple eloquence.

2 *Letters,* no. 380, 8 July 1868.

3 Her letters to American friends are glowing. There is an excision (over-discreet, perhaps) in his first letter to her.

4 They had some influence on each other. George Eliot told Mrs Lynn Lynton that she wasn't sure, if it hadn't been for Trollope, whether she could have planned *Middlemarch* on such a scale. She had a special regard for *Orley Farm*.

5 At the time when he was writing the *Autobiography* (*Auto*, p. 205), he thought her the first English novelist alive.

6 Whiting, p. 67.

7 Whiting, pp. 190–4.

8 *Letters*, no. 178, 23 August 1862.

9 Whiting, pp. 191–3.

10 *Letters*, no. 186, 3 December 1862 (from Rose to Kate Field).

11 *Letters*, no. 178, 23 August 1862 (also quoted in note 9).

15: RESIGNATION

1 *Commentary*, pp. 282 et seq.

2 Yates, *Recollections and Experience*, 2, pp. 231–2.

3 *Letters*, no. 225, 2 March 1864.

4 POR, Minutes, 15 March 1864.

5 POR, Minutes, 17 March 1864.

6 POR, Private Letter Book, John Tilley, 1 June 1864.

7 Scudamore was a creative administrator, much more so than Trollope, and introduced a whole set of reforms into the Post Office. He also wrote poetry. When he flung himself out of the Post Office, he got a job supervising the Turkish Postal Service and ended his life in a stately villa on the Black Sea.

8 POR, Minuted papers, docketed as 'Surveyors', 8 April 1864.

9 POR, Minutes, 18 April 1864.

10 POR, Minuted papers, 'Surveyors', 21 April 1864.

11 POR, Minuted papers, 'Surveyors', 8 July 1864.

12 POR, Private Letter Book, John Tilley, 9 July 1864.

13 POR, Minutes, 11 July 1864.

14 POR, Minuted papers, 'Surveyors', 18 July 1864.

15 POR, Private Letter Book, John Tilley, 10 February 1865.

16 *Letters*, no. 697, 18 April 1878.

17 Neither this letter nor the official reply appear to have survived. Trollope, with great satisfaction, includes the reply in the *Autobiography* (*Auto*, pp. 234–5).

18 It is perhaps unnecessary to observe that Sir Henry Taylor, though only a perpetual no. 3 at the Colonial Office (but with special access to the Secretary of State), was awarded a K.C.M.G. William Gregory got an automatic knighthood when he became Governor of Ceylon.

16: FATHER AND SONS

1 Gordon Haight, *George Eliot* (London, 1968), p. 335.

2 Henry provided Sadleir with a good deal of material written and oral. Henry lived to be eighty, but only survived his mother by nine years.

3 *Auto*, p. 289.

4 Enquiries have revealed that, though Trollope must have written frequently to Fred, none of these letters remains in Australia.

5 *Auto*, p. 284.

6 See above, note 4.

7 Although Trollope had to leave the house before he died, he did not correct this passage in the *Autobiography*. The manuscript had been de-posited with Henry, and wouldn't have been immediately available. Or Trollope may have forgotten some details it contained. When Henry published it, he seems to have made no amendations or corrections of any kind.

8 The only one of the Trollope houses which stays much as he knew it. It carries a plaque.

9 *Auto*, p. 292.

10 Julian Hawthorne, loc. cit.

17: CONFESSION AT SIXTY

1 *Commentary*, ch. 10.

2 *Critical Heritage* was not published until long after Sadleir's death. He could have investigated the newspaper files for himself, but, except on bibliography, his scholarship wasn't so thorough.

3 It isn't certain how well Tolstoi spoke English, but he read it with ease. The bookshelves at Yasnaya Polyana are crammed with English books, including oddities such as bound volumes of 'The Captain'. *The Prime Minister* cannot have been translated at the time Tolstoi read it, though Trollope's novels were translated more extensively into Russian than into any other language.

4 *Auto*, pp. 50–1.

18: TROLLOPE'S ART – II

1 See ch. 13.

2 Henry James used the word 'grace' about Trollope, with his usual accuracy.

3 'Absolutely', used as Trollope used it, could be heard from old men as late as the 1930s.

4 *Ulysses*, pp. 101–2.

5 Compare Edouard Dujardin, *Les Lauriers Sont Coupés* (Paris, 1887).

6 *The Small House at Allington*, ch. 7.

7 *The Small House at Allington*, ch. 17.

19: END OF A STOIC

1 *Letters*, no. 919, undated.

2 *Letters*, no. 924, undated.

3 *Letters*, nos. 866 and 867, 15 and 16 February 1882.

4 Ibid.

5 *Letters*, no. 853, 4 January 1882.

6 *Letters*, no. 905, 10 October 1882.

7 *Letters*, no. 878, 30 March 1882.

8 These letters are preserved in the Morris L. Parrish collection at Princeton (see Preface).

ILLUSTRATION ACKNOWLEDGMENTS

Page numbers set in *italic* type refer to the pages opposite the relevant colour plates. Where two numbers are given in *italic* type this refers to the double-spread colour plate between the two pages.

The photographs on pp. 22, 27, 30, *32*, *72–3*, *88–9*, *145*, *161* were taken by Derrick Witty for George Rainbird Ltd.

 2 Mansell Collection
10 Radio Times Hulton Picture Library
15 Mansell Collection
17 Reproduced by the kind permission of the Treasurer and Masters of the Bench of Lincoln's Inn
20 Mary Evans Picture Library
21 Mary Evans Picture Library
22 London Borough of Harrow Library Services
22 INSET Harrow School
24 Glasgow Art Gallery
25 Ohio Historical Society
27 London Borough of Harrow Library Services
30 TOP London Borough of Harrow Library Services
30 BOTTOM Harrow School
32 Harrow School
33 National Portrait Gallery
35 Mary Evans Picture Library
36 Mary Evans Picture Library
38 LEFT By courtesy of the Maas Gallery, London
41 By courtesy of the Post Office
44 BOTH By courtesy of the Post Office
46 By courtesy of Sotheby's, Belgravia
48 Guildhall Library, London
49 By courtesy of Sotheby's, Belgravia
50 Mansell Collection
51 LEFT Radio Times Hulton Picture Library
51 RIGHT By courtesy of Sotheby's, Belgravia
53 Mary Evans Picture Library
56–7 National Gallery of Ireland
58 Bannagher Post Office
59 BOTH By courtesy of the Post Office
61 George Morrison Productions
63 Kate Field Collection, Boston Public Library
67 BOTH George Morrison Productions
72 Victoria and Albert Museum
72–3 By courtesy of the Maas Gallery, London
73 Worcester Art Museum, Worcester, Massachusetts
74 By courtesy of the Post Office
77 ABOVE AND BELOW Winchester City Museums
77 CENTRE Mansell Collection
78 Mansell Collection
79 Salisbury and South Wiltshire Museums
81 By courtesy of Sotheby's, Belgravia
82 Reproduced by the kind permission of the Harris Museum and Art Gallery
84 Winchester City Museums
85 Mary Evans Picture Library
87 Cheshunt Public Library
88–9 Reproduced by kind permission of The Garrick Club
90 LEFT By courtesy of Arthur Ackermann & Son
90 RIGHT By courtesy of Sotheby's, Belgravia
92 LEFT Mary Evans Picture Library
92 RIGHT Radio Times Hulton Picture Library
93 LEFT Radio Times Hulton Picture Library
93 RIGHT Mary Evans Picture Library
96 The Metropolitan Museum of Art, Gift of Frederick H. Hatch, 1926
97 SCALA
99 Mansell Collection
101 Museum of the City of New York
102 ABOVE RIGHT AND BELOW In the Picture Gallery at Royal Holloway College, University of London
102 ABOVE LEFT By courtesy of Sotheby's, Belgravia
102–3 CENTRE Mansell Collection
103 ABOVE Mansell Collection

103 BELOW Rhode Island Historical Society
104–5 ALL Kate Field Collection, Boston Public Library
107 By courtesy of Sotheby's, Belgravia
108 Mary Evans Picture Library
112 ABOVE National Portrait Gallery, London
112 BELOW Reproduced by kind permission of The Garrick Club
113 Reproduced by kind permission of the Harris Museum and Art Gallery
114 BOTH By courtesy of Sotheby's, Belgravia
119 Kate Field Collection, Boston Public Library
120 Virginia Museum of Fine Arts
123 Kate Field Collection, Boston Public Library
125 Kate Field Collection, Boston Public Library
130 LEFT Mary Evans Picture Library
130 RIGHT By courtesy of the Post Office
133 By courtesy of the Post Office
133 INSET National Portrait Gallery, London
136 New York State Historical Association
136–7 Guildhall Library, London
137 National Library of Australia. Photo by courtesy of Anne-Marie Erlich
139 By courtesy of Sotheby's, Belgravia
140 National Library of Australia. Photo by courtesy of Anne-Marie Erlich
141 Photo by courtesy of Anne-Marie Erlich
143 BOTH Mary Evans Picture Library
144 By courtesy of Arthur Ackermann & Son
145 Reproduced by kind permission of the Garrick Club
146 Mansell Collection
147 Mary Evans Picture Library
149 Royal Academy of Arts, London
151 LEFT By courtesy of the Post Office
151 RIGHT Mansell Collection
155 Bristol City Art Gallery
157 Mansell Collection
160 London Museum. Photo George Rainbird Ltd
161 Sir David Scott
162 Mary Evans Picture Library
165 RIGHT By courtesy of Christie's
168 Aberdeen Art Gallery and Museum
168–9 Photo Cooper-Bridgeman Library
169 National Portrait Gallery, London
170 By courtesy of Lady Faber
171 Victoria and Albert Museum
172 LEFT City Art Gallery, Manchester
172 RIGHT National Monuments Record
174 Macmillan London Ltd
176 BOTH Radio Times Hulton Picture Library

INDEX

as impoverished barrister, 11, 16; compared with Mr Crawley, 14, 27; schizoid paranoia, 15–16, 26, 32, 33, 37; farming scheme, 16–17, 18, 19; educational plans for sons, 19–20, 21–2, 28; in America, 25, 26; increasing financial disasters, 27, 28, 34–5; literary undertaking, 33, 37; move to Bruges, 34–6, 37; death, 38

Trollope, Mrs Thomas Anthony (Frances Trollope) (mother), *33*, 40, 42, 43, 48, 60, 75, *104*; character, 14, 17–18, 63; financial reckless-ness, 18, 25, 26, 33; American scheme, 24–5, 32; reliance on Tom, 23, 28, 34, 37; neglect of Trollope, 24, 25; literary work, 32, 33, 37, 66; transports family to Bruges, 34–6,

37; occasional help to Trollope, 51; surprise at his novel-writing, 65–6, 100; in Italy, 100

Trollope, Thomas Adolphus (broth-er), 11, 15, 16, 29, 39, 51, 65, *104*, 122, 136, 167, *176*; education, 19–20, 21, 23, 28; in America, 25, 26; as sup-port for mother, 28, 34, 37; as author, 66, 100; in Italy, 100; devi-ous side, 100; Trollope's letters to, 169, 170–1

Trollope, Mrs Tom, 100, *104*

Trollopian, The, 177

Tudor, Charlie: as self-portrait, 39, 43, 85; and Civil Service examina-tion, 43–4

Ulysses (Joyce), 162–3

Verona, *102*

Vice Versa (Anstey), 173

Waltham House, *87*; Trollope's life at, 86–7, 92, 95, 129, 137; sale of, 138

War and Peace (Tolstoi), 91, 160, 162

West Indies, *102*; Trollope's Post Office work in, 96–7

Winchester, *20, 77*; Trollope's schooldays at, 20, 21, 23, 25–6, 28

Winter Thoughts about Summer Im-pressions (Dostoevsky), 182

Wortle, Dr, and choice, 111

Wright, Camilla and Frances, 24

Yates, Edmund, 39, 51, 88, 129, 132, 182